CREATING YOUR
Christian
ENGAGEMENT

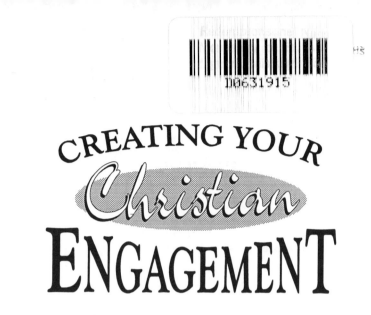

John Barry Ryan and Francis J. Lodato

LIGUORI
PUBLICATIONS

One Liguori Drive
Liguori, MO 63057-9999
(314) 464-2500

Imprimi Potest:
James Shea, C.SS.R.
Provincial, St. Louis Province
The Redemptorists

Imprimatur:
+ Edward J. O'Donnell, D.D.
Auxiliary Bishop, Archdiocese of St. Louis

ISBN 0-89243-575-5
Library of Congress Catalog Card Number: 94-76020

Cover design by Christine Kraus

TABLE OF CONTENTS

Dedication

To all the men and women who took our courses at Manhattan College, where John teaches Christian Marriage in the Religious Studies Department and Frank taught Marriage and Family Counseling in the School of Education and Human Services. Exploring relationships with our students was a work of mutual learning, lots of fun, and many surprises.

To our wives, Jeanette Ryan and Pat Lodato, who have skillfully balanced career and family responsibilities. They have brought joy to our lives, wisdom to our relationships, and wonderful mothering to our children.

SO YOU'RE GOING TO GET MARRIED!

our engagement can be the time of your life—but it's not always easy to make it so. You may find your engagement period overshadowed by the pressure to set a wedding date that is "convenient for everyone": family, friends, caterers, musicians, florist, organist, minister, jeweler, bridal and formal wear shop, printer, travel agent, your landlord-to-be, and your bosses. (Our apologies to anyone we've left out.) Quite an operation! No wonder many families hire a wedding coordinator.

All this excitement centers around the intense relationship of two people in love: you. Yet, from the moment you decide to marry, so much attention and energy is channeled in other directions. You may find that your love for each other and the relationship you are building begin to take a back seat while you coordinate all the practical details for the wedding.

Is there a more significant purpose to the engagement period than simply coordinating this most significant social event in your life? We think so. We see the engagement period as an opportunity for the two of you to deepen your relationship, explore its religious significance, and begin building a firm foundation on which years of life will stand solid.

The following chapters treat the primary aspects of your engagement period: how this time strengthens your relationship, the meaning of your wedding vows and your readiness to take them, who you are as individuals and who you are as a couple, how intimacy and sexuality deepen and strengthen your relationship, your experience of faith during your engagement, what you can do now to appreciate the significance of children becoming part of your marriage in years to come, relationship skills that will enable you to love with integrity and honesty "as long as you both shall live."

We hope that the two of you will be active readers of *Creating Your Christian Engagement*. Because this material is seriously relationship oriented, we caution you to read slowly; take your time. Together, explore your relationship and its potential to evolve into a joy-filled marriage. Create a Christian engagement that directs and supports your choices for the future. Is that too much to ask? It's up to you!

Chapter 1

BEGINNING YOUR ENGAGEMENT

obert Frost's thoughtful poem *The Road Not Taken* presents the image of two roads diverging in a yellow wood. The poetic voice says,

> *I took the one less traveled by,*
> *And that has made all the difference.*

When people reflect on the roads their lives have followed, they will often attribute significance to times of major discernment and decision making. Such times are milestones that mark a life with change; they are turning points that impact life, in one way or another, every day from that point forward.

Getting engaged and eventually getting married are such turning points in your life. As you enter this time of anticipation and excitement, we say, "Congratulations and best wishes!" We celebrate your love, your choosing of a path that will make "all the difference."

Have you noticed how songwriters compose a lot of great songs about love but very few about marriage? Love is considered romantic, exciting, and lively; marriage, however, is regarded as hard work, burdensome, perhaps even confining—"The honeymoon is over" mentality.

We don't share that view. Being a married person is one of the most exciting ways to be in life. It is every bit as romantic, exciting, and lively as love—because it is love at its best.

Married love, however, does not happen automatically. Being surrounded by married couples all your life does not automatically equip you with natural abilities to "be married."

Nor is married love an instant by-product of the marriage vows. Certainly, there is no married love without commitment, but a mere recitation of words does not ensure lifelong love.

Your Decision to Get Engaged

Your love took a giant leap when you decided to get engaged. Your mutual attraction to each other and the life experience you've shared over recent months and years have moved your friendship to a new level, one that you feel suggests marriage—so you got engaged. This is a great moment in your relationship; you will never forget it. It ushers in an entirely new period of life for the two of you. You have crossed a threshold full of promise.

You mark this decision with an engagement ring, given and accepted. This ring is a declaration of intention. It says to the world, "I want to marry; I choose to marry. Let everyone who sees this ring know that we have chosen to pursue a lifelong commitment to each other." Your decision and the symbol you use to express that decision give focus to your love. You are ready to embark on the journey of anticipating marriage, of getting to know yourselves better as individuals and as a couple, of beginning to relate with your respective families in new and exciting ways.

The Catholic Church has a blessing for your engagement that can be celebrated by both your families, perhaps at a meal together. If the two of you have not yet received this blessing, you can arrange it with your parents. The blessing underlines your love for each other, your need for God's grace, and the importance of your engagement as a time of preparation for marriage. The blessing of the engaged couple is short and appropriate:

> *We praise you, Lord,*
> *for your gentle plan draws together*
> *your children,*
> *in love for each other.*
> *Strengthen their hearts,*
> *so that they will keep faith with each other,*
> *please you in all things,*
> *and so come to the happiness of celebrating*
> *the sacrament of their marriage.*
> *We ask this through Christ, our Lord.*
> **Amen.**

This blessing allows you and your parents to bring to your engagement a family and a religious dimension. In this way, your engagement is not simply an individual act that somehow has its place outside the framework of the family and the wedding liturgy. The engagement blessing gives your parents a role that properly belongs to them: the blessing of your love for each other. It weaves your relationship into the fabric of your families and your faith.

Celebrating the blessing in the context of a meal gives both your families a chance to begin overcoming any feelings of awkwardness, if these exist. It is an opportunity for your families to acknowledge, with hope and promise, that they are being connected by the bridge of your marriage. If your parents have reservations about your engagement and pending marriage, the engagement blessing is a chance for them to place their concerns in God's keeping while expressing support for your choice.

When you get engaged, your families may experience mixed feelings of joy, sadness, and hope: joy as they recognize the happiness you experience in your relationship; sadness as they adjust to a new stage in their relationship with you; hope as they look ahead to the adventure the two of you are about to enter. The engagement blessing ritualizes these very human emotions.

If you are an interreligious couple, you will appreciate the dignity and respect the engagement blessing bestows on your individual faith traditions. It expresses the hope and faith of all those who are genuinely interested in your happiness and the success of your union.

The Engagement Period

What do you "do" during your engagement period? What should you "accomplish"?

A popular bridal magazine offers a list that details eighty tasks that need attention in the process of planning the ceremony, reception, and honeymoon. It is a daunting agenda. Many of these tasks are important—even necessary. Moving through the list, checking off each item as it's completed, you experience a great sense of relief and accomplishment. This endeavor, however, does not constitute what you "do" as you "create your Christian engagement." These details do not focus on the more important tasks that your commitment to engagement has set up for your interpersonal relationship which are:

- Expressing your serious respect for each other as unique and precious persons
- Showing each other that you are trustworthy
- Exploring your understanding of "commitment" and how you intend to live life "committed" to each other

Welcome these tasks, and take them seriously; they are the first layers in the foundation of your marital relationship. As an engaged couple, you are going to continue to get to know each other's strengths and weaknesses; you are going to grow, emotionally and intellectually. Since you are going to be asked to give more of yourself than you have ever given before, the sincerity of your declarations of love are going to be tested. That is what you "do" during this time: you develop your capacities for relating to each other.

Typically, the engagement period lasts six months to a year, sometimes longer. Because engagement is a time of heightened interaction within your relationship, the two of you are drawn closer together. Some couples sail through this period of heightened interaction without any problems, enjoying a newfound sense of mutuality, intimacy, and trust. Others experience a great deal of confusion, pain, and doubt that either strengthens the relationship or leads the couple to reconsider their commitment. For good reason, then, the engagement period cannot be rushed.

Marriage Preparation

As part of your preparation for marriage, your pastor will arrange for the two of you to complete a marriage-preparation instrument: a tool that the two of you can use to assess the areas of strength and weakness in your relationship. The instrument covers the main issues that are crucial to a sound and healthy relationship. With the aid of this tool, the two of you are better equipped to talk about your relationship with the pastor.

You will also be offered a choice of several marriage-preparation programs. Engaged Encounter, Pre-Cana conferences, and sponsor-couple programs are the most widely used. Engaged Encounter is a weekend experience; a small group of engaged couples meet with a team composed of a priest and two married couples. The team helps the couples explore and talk about crucial marital areas, such as those we address here, and practical matters, such as finances.

Pre-Cana conferences are usually one-day events with a large group of engaged couples. The agenda covers the same crucial areas as the Engaged Encounter weekend, but with less intensity.

Sponsor-couple programs involve married couples who invite engaged couples into their homes to discuss the important issues related to marriage.

Each of these allows you to meet others who know what you're going through, who can help you identify the strengths and weaknesses in your relationship, who can help you take a hard look at difficult issues, and who can provide you with the time and space and support you need to do this important task. See what programs are available in your diocese, talk it over, and decide which one you feel is best for your relationship.

Your Engagement: More Than a Testing Ground

Your engagement period tests your conviction about the life you expect to share—but it's much more than a testing ground. This period of your life is a grace-filled opportunity to deepen your relationship. You learn to express your serious respect for each other as unique and precious persons; you show each other that you are trustworthy; you explore your understanding of commitment. These are the tasks before you. Embracing these tasks is the beginning of a joy-filled, satisfying, and enduring marriage.

There are many ways to take on these tasks of engagement. To set the tone right from the beginning, however, take a close look at the marriage vows. These vows sum up the basic dispositions of persons who are, indeed, mature and aware of the life they are about to begin creating. A consideration of them at the beginning of your engagement will set you off on the right direction.

Reflecting Together

Separately, list your concerns about your relationship or the years ahead. Set a time when you will have no interruptions, and compare your lists. Empathy for each other's concerns is the key here.

Chapter 2

UNDERSTANDING THE MEANING OF YOUR VOWS

T he marriage vows you are preparing to profess will be a turning point in your life and a foundation for your marriage. Everything leads up to your vows and everything flows from them. Without vows, there is no bedrock to your relationship. Without the public declaration and mutual exchange of your vows, there is no marriage.

All marriage rites focus on and celebrate your mutual giving and taking, and many customs highlight this exchange.

You will join your right hands while you profess your vows at the wedding ceremony; you will feed each other a piece of wedding cake; perhaps you'll kiss every time the guests clink their glasses with a piece of silverware. These traditional rituals celebrate what the exchange of marriage vows signifies: your giving and taking of each other.

In the Catholic Church's wedding liturgy, there are two forms for your exchange of consent. One form involves each of you saying "I take you to be my wife (husband). I promise to be true to you in good times and in bad, in sickness and in health. I will love you and honor you all the days of my life." The other form is a question-and-answer format. The priest will present each of you with a question to which you respond, "I do."

The traditional English form of the nuptial vows has a rhythmic movement to it: "I take you for my lawful husband (wife), to have and to hold, from this day forward, for better, for worse, for richer, for poorer, in sickness and in health, until death do us part."

A recent ecumenical rite for spouses from different Christian churches instructs each spouse to say, "In the presence of God and this community, I take you to be my wife (husband); to have and to hold from this day forward, in joy and in sorrow, in plenty and in want, in sickness and in health, to love and to cherish, as long as we both shall live. This is my solemn vow."

As you can see, these Christian marriage rites place an emphasis on a total giving of self—no restrictions. You make a promise for a future about which you know very little except that there will be good times and bad times, joy and sorrow, and sickness and health. You literally leap into the unknown, guided principally by your love for each other, your respect for your relationship, and your faith. Totally and completely, you trust that everything will work out.

Getting Ready to Make These Promises

It has been said that we spend more time and effort buying a house than we do choosing the person we marry. It seems buying a house is an intentional act, but choosing a spouse and creating a mutually satisfying life together somehow takes care of itself.

And think of the way you prepare yourself for a profession or trade. You apply your time, efforts, and resources to acquire a skill that will enable you to earn a living and secure a lifestyle you're comfortable with. Even during your childhood, your parents may have created a college fund for your ongoing education, and aunts and uncles probably asked "What do you want to be when you grow up?" All this played a major role in the way you were socialized for earning a living and developing to your fullest human potential.

On the other hand, how have each of you prepared yourselves for marriage? While falling in love may be wonderful, it's how you live your marriage that will count.

Your exchange of consent indicating your intentions to give and take each other every day of your life is a serious gesture. The Church recognizes that and offers you a great deal of guidance and support during your engagement. Many dioceses have a six-month waiting period between the time you approach the parish about your wedding and the actual ceremony itself. In addition to a series of meetings with your pastor, most dioceses also have an obligatory policy about attendance at a marriage-preparation program. These practices and policies highlight the importance of the engagement as a time of intense preparation for marriage.

A successful marriage-preparation program will prepare you to continue on the road toward marriage—or to see that you should not marry at this particular time or this particular person.

Vows: The Beginning of a Vocation

To be "called" to something means that you are going to live your life a certain way. This is a vocation. It takes a lot of maturity and faith to choose a vocation.

Marriage is a vocation. Explore the meaning of vocation, especially marriage. What does it mean to you? Why do you think you're "called" to the vocation of marriage—especially with each other? Because vows mark your entry into the vocation of marriage, they deserve your careful attention and prayerful consideration. Certainly, you have a general idea of what marriage requires; you have ample opportunities to witness the love and dedication of married couples every day. But the marriage vows give you a sense of what characterizes the calling to marriage: mutual fidelity, honor, and love. This is the simple—and profound—meaning of the marriage vows: "I will be true to you....I will love and honor you all the days of my life."

"I Will Be True to You"

"I will be true to you" means a lot more than love songs convey. If you are called to be "true," to be faithful, you are a person who understands and respects the meaning of fidelity. You are a person who can be trusted and who can trust others.

What does *trust* and *trustworthiness* mean? How does trust "look"? Trust does not contradict itself; actions match words, words match actions. A trustworthy person completes tasks with honesty and integrity, respects rules and laws and does not cheat, lie, or make empty promises, does not make excuses for mistakes and failures, and is not two-faced in dealing with others.

The other side of being trustworthy is the ability to trust. A person who trusts has a healthy sense of self-worth, respects the personhood of others, and believes in the basic goodness of others.

Trust and trustworthiness—fidelity—in marriage is not an abstract concept but a lifeline of health for your relationship. Throughout the years of your marriage, fidelity will be most crucial in your sexual expressions of love. That is why sexual infidelity is so devastating to your relationship—because a major lifeline of health has been cut off.

Sexual exchanges in marriage are your most intense expressions of total self-giving and receiving in body, mind, spirit, and soul; it is an expression of fully committed love. Your marriage bed is more than a piece of furniture; it is the sacred place where you communicate your deepest self to each other. Your mutual sexual desires and sexual fulfillment serve to deepen your commitment as a couple.

Small wonder, then, that "cheating on your spouse" does such damage to marriage. Your total and mutual self-giving is dealt a savage blow when one of you withdraws the promise to be faithful. Your sexual expressions become shallow, like a consumer commodity, subject to all the laws of consumerism.

You prepare for sexual fidelity in marriage by being sexually faithful now, during your engagement period. Your engagement announcement tells everyone—including yourselves—that you are exclusively committed to each other. You both stop looking for a future mate because you believe you've found the person with whom you wish to spend your life. Fidelity during your engagement period is expressed in gestures of affection that the two of you reserve for each other exclusively, gestures that reflect the deep and common bond you are building.

Fidelity is also reflected in other special things that the two of you share, like a special song, place, or flavor of ice cream that you call "ours." These and other choices bind you together and form part of the fabric of the mutual, faithful relationship you are building.

Your choice to get engaged, however, can have unexpected consequences that challenge your fidelity.

Jane thought that Charley should have gotten engaged to her and not to Alice. As a result, Jane is angry with Charley and wants nothing to do with Alice. Jane thinks that Charley led her on—and intends to tell Alice all about it.

Phil feels that George "stole" Linda from him and that Linda doesn't know what a two-faced guy George is. He wants to get Linda alone to tell her the "truth" about George.

Wayne and Theo kid their best friend, Jamal, who just got engaged to Latisha: "She leads you around by the nose," they insist. As a response, Jamal feels like he has to prove his independence by disagreeing with Latisha in front of his friends.

Audrey, jealous of Sue's engagement to Fred, plots to get Fred alone and make Sue jealous.

At a beach party, Lester plans to show Laura that he's more of a man than her fiancé.

These are not mere soap-opera plots that threaten mutual fidelity; these situations come up all the time—and bring tremendous pressure to bear on a relationship. Perhaps you've already been exposed to such plots. When confronted by outside attacks, fidelity means you put your relationship first. Together, with respect for each other, you decide how to deal with people's negative reactions to your engagement. You do not hide the situation from each other; you do not try to take care of things by yourself. Trying to solve these kinds of problems on your own, without relying on your beloved's perspective and wisdom, is to create a secret in your relationship from the beginning—and secrets have a way of eroding trust and trustworthiness. Secretive behavior leads to evasive behavior that leads to difficult questions—which can end up in lies. This is not fidelity.

Fidelity can also be threatened from within your relationship. Perhaps you've already discovered, for example, that being engaged does not automatically "protect" you from pain; you still hurt each other's feelings; you have misunderstandings; you disappoint each other. This kind of pain does not indicate that your relationship is weak. Contrary to the popular slogan, being in love means you *will often* say "I'm sorry." That's part of the reality of an intimate bond. When you hurt each other during your engagement, don't pout, don't keep score, don't give each other the "cold shoulder," don't seek consolation in the arms of someone "more understanding." Fidelity now, during your engagement period, and throughout your entire married life, means that you face the pain together. The two of you pinpoint the pain, talk about what it feels like and where it comes from, and deal with it together—honestly and faithfully.

As an engaged couple, you build a foundation for your marriage that is mutually enriching, where forgiveness and reconciliation form part of your relationship. Choosing each other and entering into the engagement period is a time of great personal growth; it introduces you to a radically new dimension of life that can allow for positive change.

"I Will Love You"

Now that you are engaged, note how your parents' sexual love is surrounded by numerous acts of love that extend to the whole of their marriage. Notice how routine and mundane activities, such as doing laundry, shopping for food, mowing the lawn, cleaning the house, preparing meals, washing the car, and taking out the garbage, are all part of deep married love. These daily chores, performed carefully and deliberately, are statements of love; they take on a profoundly intimate significance.

Unfortunately, intimacy in this culture has become synonymous with sex, which is a misrepresentation. What characterizes intimacy is mutual attention, affection, care, and communication. Sexual intimacy is the total expression of this more encompassing understanding of intimacy that always seeks what is best for the other. When you recognize this larger notion of intimacy, you are capable of sustaining a loving relationship. And in the midst of the routine is where the two of you prepare yourselves to love in this encompassing way.

Many people look upon engagement as the end of the chase and, therefore, the end of the excitement in the relationship. If in fact, you are "creating your Christian engagement," this will not be true for the two of you. You will experience your love for each other during this time much the same as you will experience your love throughout your married life. You will enjoy periods of excitement and periods of routine—and believe it or not, it will be to your advantage if you know more routine than excitement. It is in routine that you have the opportunity to see each other's individuality, the real person you love.

The part of your vows that state "I will love you" also have significant spiritual implications as well. One of the prefaces of the marriage liturgy says, "The love of man and woman is made holy in the sacrament of marriage, and becomes the mirror of [God's] everlasting love." This statement reveals something of the vocation of marriage. To each other, to your children, to your families, friends, and neighbors, your marriage is a visible expression of God's love in the world. You are symbols of God's love for God's creation and of Christ's love for the Church.

This is true during your engagement period as well; the two of you, in the love you share, mirror God's love—to each other and to the world. In loving each other, you glimpse something of the mystery of love that is at the heart of the universe. Your love for each other repeats the wisdom of the prophets: we are created by Love to love. The love that characterizes your engagement reminds us of the vital and powerful force that love is; the full development of all human potential rests in love.

Prior to this point in your lives, your experiences of loving have been somewhat circumstantial. For example, love for your parents is largely a result of circumstances: your parents raised you, cared for you, nourished you through the years. The love between the two of you, however, is different. It is a love freely given, freely received, without any circumstantial history. This act of committing yourself to each other mirrors the Creator's commitment to humankind, collectively and individually. God loves the world; God loves each of you. You now experience this love personally in and through your shared love. By your act of commitment to love freely, you engage in an activity that has God as its source.

Love seeks union and communion with the beloved; that is the nature of love. This search for union, like your love for each other, mirrors the desired union and communion among all persons. According to Catholic teaching, this is the work of the Holy Spirit. Your engagement relationship puts you in touch with your desire for union and communion; it leads you gradually to a deeper investment in each other's lives.

Your relationship makes demands of you; it calls you to give of yourself and to make sacrifices for each other. This self-giving, even when it hurts, prepares you for deeper giving in the full marital commitment.

These characteristics of your love introduce you, perhaps as never before, into the mystery of life and the meaning of love. They can help deepen your understanding of what you are professing with the words "I will love you." Perhaps, too, you have a deeper appreciation for the Church's attention to the living God and why she values so deeply and celebrates tirelessly the life, death, and resurrection of Jesus Christ, who exemplified a life of love.

"I Will Honor You"

To honor a person is to esteem a person. To honor a person is not to belittle or embarrass that person. We honor a person when we don't attempt to control his or her actions, thoughts, and values.

Unfortunately, to honor is not easy; we've all failed to honor those we love. As part of growing up and learning to survive, we are socialized with techniques that help us cope with life's trials. When we use these coping techniques as means to control others, we fail to honor. Consider the following example of a failure to honor.

Roy uses Janice, his date, as the butt of jokes for the entertainment of others. Roy is controlling Janice; he's setting himself up to survive at all cost. When Janice objects, Roy can defend himself by saying, "Hey, it's just teasing. There's no harm in a little fun." If Janice continues to object, Roy can shift the blame by accusing Janice of not having a sense of humor. When

Janice points out that this is unfair, Roy can use a false apology; he can acknowledge that he may have been insensitive or inappropriate and ask Janice to be a good sport in accepting his apology. If Janice does, Roy is off the hook with virtually little concern about doing the same thing again sometime. If Janice spots this weapon and insists that Roy acknowledge her pain and assure her that it won't happen again, Roy can resort to his last and ultimate weapon: anger. If he can yell loud enough and swear with the right emphasis, accusing Janice of being unreasonable— even unforgiving—then he might possibly get away with the whole thing.

When you honor each other, you do not resort to the weapons you've picked up along the way in the survival-at-any-cost game. As you prepare for marriage, cultivate honor between you. Mutual disarmament deepens your relationship; it replaces instinctive survival with thoughtfulness and unconditional love.

It is helpful to remember the distinction between treating each other as persons and treating each other as objects. When you treat each other as objects, you serve your own personal needs while disregarding the personhood of your beloved.

You do not honor each other if you let your emotions have free reign between you. The level of exclusive intimacy you are cultivating during this time does not give you license to be abusive. This, again, is treating each other as objects and not as persons who have a right to be respected and loved. Physical abuse—of any kind and to any degree—is a red flag that should call a halt to any relationship.

When you were small, you may have been taught to count to ten before saying something hurtful in anger. This is a good exercise, but take it one step further. When you are upset with your beloved, count ten, and while you're counting, think of the precious goodness of your partner, of the attractive qualities that you find especially appealing. That human being does not deserve abusive words or actions from you—or anyone. If you catch yourself saying things like "If you were a real man...," "I never met anybody as jealous as you," "You're neurotic," or any other common putdown, you're not honoring your beloved. You're not taking seriously the depth of the vows you intend to pronounce.

Positively honoring each other means that you express appreciation, courtesy, concern, and high regard for each other. You affirm each other's strengths, you are patient and supportive of each other's weaknesses, and you assume full responsibility for your own actions and emotions. To some extent, the golden rule illustrates what we mean by honoring each other: "Do unto others as you would have others do unto you." This convention is built on your own individual sense of self-worth and a deep appreciation for the value of your partner. From a gospel perspective, it means valuing yourself and your beloved because you've both been created by God and are destined for a loving relationship with God.

Contract and Covenant

The exchange of consent with the desire to create a partnership for life with another person is called the "marriage contract." Throughout history, this contract has been accompanied by prenuptial and nuptial agreements, always with the purpose of seeing to the welfare of one or both of the spouses during the marriage or in the event that the marriage ends in divorce. These legal aspects of marriage are dictated by custom or, in more celebrated contemporary cases, by the personal desires of individuals who have large amounts of property.

While the legal aspects of marriage are important and everyone should understand them, there is another important aspect to the exchange of consent that deserves careful consideration: sacramentality. In a Christian marriage, the sacramental and covenantal dimensions of marriage are significant.

The word *covenant* is connected to biblical tradition. In the Hebrew Scriptures, God enters a covenant with Israel. Covenant refers to the strength of commitment in the relationship between God and God's people, who are bound together in mutual fidelity. In the Christian Scriptures, Jesus' disciples used the concept of covenant in connection with Jesus' death. At the Last Supper, Jesus said of the cup of wine he was going to share with his disciples, "This is the new covenant sealed by my blood" (1 Corinthians 11:25). The continued use of covenant language at the Eucharist underlines the strong ties that bind Christians to Jesus' life, death, and resurrection.

Understanding marriage as a covenant, the Church respects these profound traditions. The Church puts your exchange of promises to each other in the larger context of God's commitment to Israel and Jesus' commitment to his own community and, indeed, to all men and women. This association shows how seriously the Church takes the marital union of its members. In the eyes of the Church, you will be for each other as God was for Israel and as Israel was for God, as Jesus is for the Church and as the Church is for Jesus. Although there is sin and imperfection in Israel and in the Church, they never abandon God but return always to repentance. For their part, God and Jesus never abandon their chosen spouses. They are united as lovers. Nuptial imagery aptly describes their relationship.

Your engagement period, marked by a myriad of practical concerns, offers you an opportunity to discover the meaning of marriage as a covenant. The engagement ring, the wedding rings, the minister, the place for the wedding, the music, the honeymoon site, all require planning and judgment—and everyone is curious about these details. For example, when you show your engagement ring to others, invariably, someone will ask about carats, cut, even cost. Swimming in these practical concerns, you may find it difficult to reflect on the spiritual dimensions of your relationship. Yet, the Church and the Church's liturgy always invite you to see beyond the material to the spiritual, to see the spiritual dimension that inhabits the material world.

To get at the covenant dimensions in your relationship, consider the following questions: Why do I love this person I plan to marry? Why does he or she love me? What has this person helped me to understand about myself and my faith? How does our love for each other make us better people? make the world a better place? These questions reveal the spiritual dimensions of your engaged relationship; they give you a sense of what it means to live marriage as a covenant.

One of the readings in the Church's wedding lectionary is Jesus' comments about salt and light: "You are salt to the world....You are light for the world" (Matthew 5:13,14). The disciples of Christ are called to point to that reality with unselfish love for others, with openness to the poor and the least among us, and with forgiveness. As a married couple, you will live your baptismal vocation within a covenanted relationship. The two of you will create a partnership to form a Christian household, and within your household, you will be called to create an environment that exemplifies peace and justice.

Knowing what this vocation entails in both its material and spiritual dimensions gives you a sense of what should be going on in your relationship as an engaged couple. Although it's easy to focus on the practical details of your wedding day, you cannot remain silent about the details of the lifelong covenant you are planning to enter. When you're tempted to censor some of your thoughts and concerns, don't. When you know within what bothers you or inspires you, find the words to express yourselves and welcome the risk that creates in your relationship. This is the preparation demanded of those entering a covenant. Granted, this is not easy; it's never easy to move from banter to profundity or from the practical to the spiritual. But it is not out of your reach to probe the religious dimensions of Christian marriage. Discuss your reasons for getting married in the Church, your understanding of what it means to say that marriage is a sacrament, and how you intend to make your household reflect the essential gospel teachings: love for God and love for your neighbor.

When you discuss these things, don't consider your comments as final answers or cut-in-stone perspectives. Your discussions are only starting points that lead you to discover your deepest convictions.

The simple words of consent at your wedding are loaded with meaning; their implications are staggering. Maybe, as with many of the most challenging things in life, you prefer not to think about these implications. They might make you hesitate and ask, "Who can live up to them? Can I? Can we?" A more appropriate question is "What can we do *now* so that when we pronounce our marriage vows, we will understand them and welcome the promise and the challenge they imply?"

The marriage vows place before you the path you are to follow together. Despite the great difficulty people experience in living up to their marriage vows, the vows are not unrealistic; they do not promote an illusory view of life's possibilities. Rather, the vows establish the mutually understood keystones to a life-giving relationship with another person: be faithful to that person, love that person, and honor that person in all situations always. And when you fail, do not delay reconciliation.

During your engagement period, you are learning to live these promises. Once you marry, your unique relationship will provide the details for how the vows are to be lived on a day-today basis. You will find that the vows you profess on your wedding day are not starry-eyed notions, romantic ideals, or impossible demands. Rather, they are the contours of a life system within which your Christian marriage will flourish.

Prayer During Your Engagement

Prayer, which allows you to get in touch with God, is most relevant for you as an engaged couple. As you grow more intimate with each other, as you take time for your relationship, and as you begin to form your life as a couple, bring your discoveries and concerns to prayer. Rather than resorting to prayer when things get hard and disappointing, daily prayer now, during your engagement, opens you to the grace that will be yours throughout the ever-deepening sacrament of your marriage.

Make prayer a part of your relationship: ponder Scripture, hold your mutual concerns for yourselves and others in a common spirit of prayer, worship together on a regular basis. Pray together, aloud or silently; be direct and formal about your prayer or be indirect and casual. Pray while you're apart. Thank God for each other's goodness, gifts, and love. Praise God for the love that you experience in each other's arms. Pray over problems; pray over joys. Pray about your insecurities, your hesitations, your fears. Bring all praise and gratitude, all needs and concerns, to God. Praying for your relationship now and for your hopes and dreams will give focus to your marriage.

The Church Needs You

The overriding characteristic of your engagement is joy— a joy that is witnessed by your family, friends, and faith community. During your engagement, the newness, excitement, and freshness of your relationship mirrors the newness, excitement, and freshness that Jesus brought into the world. In fact, Jesus was often described as a bridegroom and, like a bridegroom, he brought fresh joy to a world grown cynical, tired, and discouraged.

Today, still, the world needs joy—and the two of you have that to offer; you display the deepest possibilities of personal and communal growth. A Church that loves to see herself in marital imagery as the bride of Christ needs lovers—engaged lovers—to remind the faithful that it is forever renewed, forever fresh, as it waits for the fulfillment of the kingdom.

As chapter 8, verse 7, in the Song of Songs puts it, "Many waters cannot quench love, no flood can sweep it away." When lovers flourish and revel in their commitment to each other, they reveal to all of us the truth of this Scripture passage. Your initial knowing of each other, growing attraction, and deepening intimacy have led you into each other's interior lives. When this leads you to a greater commitment to and care for each other, you create an indestructible love relationship. You are responding to the call to a vocation: marriage. And what a wonderful calling it is!

Reflecting Together

What does the phrase "fidelity in a relationship" mean to each of you? Discuss your answers. Try to understand the factors that influence your interpretation of fidelity. Understanding is important here, not confrontation.

Intimacy means permitting someone to enter into your psychological space. What does intimacy mean to each of you? How do you each experience intimacy?

Honoring each other is an important aspect of your engagement and marriage. How have your parents honored each other? How have you honored each other during your courtship and engagement? How do you plan to honor each other throughout your marriage?

Chapter 3

GETTING TO KNOW ME

"I promise." These are the first words of your wedding vows. There is no better way to consider your readiness for marriage than with a thorough evaluation of your "I." After all is said and done, if *you* do not get to know *you* intimately and objectively, you may be impeded in your ability to get to know someone else.

Beginning the Process of Self-Discovery

You should not be a constant source of surprise to yourself. Rather, you should be in the process of continually getting to know new facets of your personality, new insights into your drives and attitudes. With these new levels of self-understanding, you develop a value system that will sustain you throughout your entire life. Recalling your past, learning from your mistakes, growing with wisdom and age, all help you realize the changes taking place within you every day of your life. You begin to recognize your needs and become aware of your behavioral patterns.

Is getting to know yourself easy? Well, yes and no. It's difficult if you deny some of the parts of yourself that are painful to look at. It's easy if you're honest with yourself about your strengths and weaknesses, without trying to deny anything. Getting to know yourself is also easier if you keep an open mind and are willing to probe deeply into yourself to find the causes and motivations that explain your behavior.

Throughout the process of self-discovery, remember that who you are now did not happen overnight. Some of the current *you* is the result of heredity; some of *you* results from the environment you grew up in; some of *you* depends upon the way you reacted to the environment. Are you the oldest sibling in the family? the youngest? the only child? the only male? the only female? It makes a difference. You've had no control over these things, and understanding this makes it easier for you to get to know more about yourself.

More than just your family composition, however, contributed to who you are today. How you related with each of your parents, siblings, and extended family members influenced you through the years. Your ethnic background and socioeconomic experience also formed you, your value system, your faith, and your world view. Don't deny the impact any of these elements have had. Try to understand your present self in the light of these factors. One of the positive lessons we learned from the sixties is to admit our origins, to be proud of what went into us, and to acknowledge and respect the cultural heritage that preceded us. Mottoes and slogans like "Proud to be Puerto Rican," "Black Power," and "Kiss me, I'm Italian" all told a single story from that decade: the diversity of the human race is to be celebrated! This appreciation paved the way for the present-day emphasis on multiculturalism.

In the process of considering all the aspects of your history that have contributed to the person you are today, don't hesitate to add the negative experiences. Friends, parents, relatives, teachers, coaches, and countless incidents have impacted you, from time to time, in a negative way. That is not to say that blame needs be leveled at any person(s) or event(s). Rather, considering the negative experiences is part of a thorough and honest inventory of your history—which helps you understand who you are today.

Do you see the complicated maze out of which your personality has developed? Add to that, of course, the genes that were transmitted to you and the choices you've made in each situation along the way. How can the journey to better self-understanding be made easier given this endless list of influences?

Like any journey, your efforts should be well thought out and well planned. Even with careful planning, however, your journey will not be one of familiar paths; rather, it is replete with side roads and detours not seen or anticipated. There are, nonetheless, guidelines that can make the journey safer and friendlier.

Openness and Honesty

The journey of self-discovery must be tread with openness and honesty. As you go down the road, you must be willing to take in all the sights. Some you will like and enjoy; others will give you reason to pause, to interpret the meaning of what you see. Openness and honesty means that you truly look into yourself to find out why you do what you do, what has meaning for you, what makes you happy, what makes you sad, what motivates you, and what facets of your behavior you don't like.

Start with a subjective assessment of your personality. Sit in front of a mirror, and describe in detail the person you see there. Look deeply into yourself, and develop a composite personality picture. If the profile you develop is too one-sided, that is, you can't find anything good to say about yourself or you can't find anything that needs improvement, you haven't been open and honest with yourself. You've either been too severe or too easy on yourself. Remember, an integrated personality includes strengths that can be built upon and weaknesses that have the potential to become strengths.

Consider your triumphs and disappointments. Ask yourself about your goals in life. Do you know what they are, where they come from, and how important they are to you? What are you willing to sacrifice to achieve these goals? What will happen if you don't achieve them? Are they realistic goals for you? Are they achievable? Do you have a good sense of what achieving these goals can mean for your happiness? for the happiness of the person you plan to marry? Can you establish a priority among your goals?

Do you like yourself? Do you like your general attitude toward life? your lifestyle? your daily routine? After all is said and done, are you okay with *you*?

After you've investigated these questions and have some idea of where you are subjectively, you are on the way to learning about your real self. What you see begins to help round out the larger picture of just who you are and how you came to be who you are.

Self-evaluation can be fun; it can also be painful. It can help you discover things you suspected about yourself but could never really understand. For the first time, you may be forced to admit some aspects of yourself that you would rather not admit or accept. With openness and honesty, and with God's help, you can face yourself—and most of us come out looking better than we expected. It's worth the risk. The benefits are great.

You might also want to learn a little about your ideal self and how you would like others to think about you. If your real self and your ideal self are about equal, you're probably pretty satisfied with life. If the real self drags behind where and what you would like to be, this may take some repairing.

List the areas in which you think your real self falls short. Then judge whether your ideal self is a realistic, achievable goal for you. If you determine that it is, start working on those areas in the real self that you want to improve. Take them one at a time; gradually, the distance between your real self and your ideal self will begin to close.

Along your journey of self-examination, take a look at your social self: the way others see you. This will give you insight into your interpersonal relationships. It will help you understand the way people react to you and why. Again, if your real self, your ideal self, and your social self are compatible, then you should be a fairly contented person. If people see you as being different from the way you want to be seen, then you have work to do. For example, when you think you're being humorous and others find you obnoxious, you have work to do! Unfortunately, you can't distribute a personal guidebook that helps others understand who you are, but you can question your friends about how they see you. Their insights may come as a surprise to you; their comments may be exactly what you expected. All these pieces help you understand *you*.

Your Relationships

Now that you know yourself a little better, wouldn't it be great to know how you interact with a variety of other persons? How important this is to marriage cannot be overemphasized. After all, Christian marriage is an intimate and profound relationship, freely entered into by two consenting adults of the opposite sex, for the mutual comfort and satisfaction of the people entering into the union and for the procreation and rearing of children. Christian marriage is characterized by the willingness of the partners to understand, love, and support each other. When you enter into this union, you ask that it be sanctified by God, and you intend it to last a lifetime.

It makes sense, then, to look into yourself to see how you form, maintain, and enjoy relationships. Remember, you enter into relationships for a variety of reasons. Some relationships are entered into because you are attracted to something in the personality of another person. It may be the person's wit, looks, intelligence, compassion, empathy, understanding, manner of speaking, religious convictions, talents, or value system. What constitutes the positive pull others have on you? When you know that, you'll begin to understand your own requirements in establishing a relationship.

You may find that not all of your motives are noble, however. A woman, for example, may be lonely, and one of her male friends is available. He might not be her first choice to spend time with, but he is present and willing to be with her, and she takes advantage of the opportunity to compensate for her loneliness.

If you view relationships according to their utilitarian value, that is, how you can use them for some personal end, you need to rethink the entire experience of interpersonal relating. What value do you place on relationships? Why do you enter into relationships in the first place? Who are some of your friends and why are they special? Are you attracted to them for their own personhood or for some other reason that serves your needs?

How you view relationships and enter into them has a lot to do with the role modeling you received from your parents and other significant persons in your formative years. If you observed others in relationships of convenience, and if true friendship was not evident, you may have come to treat relationships lightly. In some cases, it will take considerable time to refashion healthy standards of relating.

You may also discover that you've been fickle in your relationships through the years. Perhaps you've been attracted to one person one day and someone else the next. Certainly, all of us need a variety of people among our friends, but this need should have some staying power attached to it. Do you enter relationships carefully or do you pick up and discard friends at random? Do you understand the pain of being discarded as a friend? Do you care for the feelings of others? Are you sensitive in your relationships? How do you distinguish between friendships and acquaintances?

If you treat people as if they are disposable commodities, you will not be able to attain the depth of love and respect required in marriage. Discover what relationships mean to you. Consider several specific characteristics that determine a deep and lasting friendship for you and a relationship that is less intense. What pulls you in the direction of cultivating a meaningful relationship? Why?

How Does This Relate to Marriage?

In this process of getting to know *you*, you've considered two basic questions: "Who am I?" and "How do I relate to others?"

If you've been open and honest with yourself in this process, you're beginning to understand yourself and your need for other people. How does this relate to you as an engaged person who is planning to marry?

The more completely you know yourself, the easier it is to understand why you do what you do, why you say what you say, and why you feel the way you do about issues, people, and events. If you know yourself, you understand your value system, your moral character, your faith. You begin to understand the meaning of your life—perhaps the meaning of all life. Obviously, you will not have all the answers for leading a meaningful life, but you will know what is important to you and why.

If you're at this point, you are no doubt at peace with yourself. You don't wish for things you can't have or achieve, you accept the realities of your particular life circumstances, and you understand what drives and satisfies you. For example, if you're not as tall as you'd like to be and you accept that fact, your self-concept is sound. You know *you* and you appreciate *you*. You know that you're not the center of the universe. You are aware of yourself and others as children of God.

With this understanding, you are better equipped to consider the vocation of marriage—because you know yourself. You know if you're capable of entering into a union that requires sacrifice, understanding, and unqualified acceptance of another person. Having accomplished all this, you're ready to get to know your partner.

Before you begin that process, let's consider a detour, as we mentioned before. Suppose that in the process of getting to know yourself, you conclude that you cannot be giving, that sacrifice for another person is not one of your gifts, that compromising what you want in the moment is too much to ask. What can you learn from this? One conclusion is evident: to attempt marriage at this stage of your life would be unwise for you and a tremendous disservice to your partner. If you think your attitudes can be altered, then postponing marriage might be a temporary state. One caution here, however. If the picture you have painted of yourself is fairly accurate, it will not change overnight because you meet someone who sweeps you off your feet. Infatuation is not a firm base for marriage.

If you come up with a self-profile that makes marriage risky at this point, continue to examine yourself. What influences your attitudes today? What has helped form your attitudes over the years? What motivates you? What's important to you? Money? power? prestige? comfort? security? freedom? commitment? religion? God? You may want to consider "outside" input through this process. Speaking to someone who has the training and insight to help you understand your motivations is a worthwhile investment. The more accepting you are of yourself and the more secure you are, the easier it will be for you to be assertive, to be cognizant of the parameters of behavior within which you are able to function comfortably.

Self-evaluation—honest personal reflection—is the only way to reach a clear image of yourself. Knowing what you value and why you value it helps you form a self-profile that enables you to make mature choices. Introspection helps you learn if you're capable of the kind of commitment that constitutes marriage. Marriage requires give and take. If you are not ready to give, you are not ready for marriage.

Nora looked beautiful in her wedding dress as she stood with her family in the entrance hall of the church. She felt uneasy. "I'm not sure I want to go through with this," she choked. "I want to call it off." Nora's patient and sympathizing parents assured her that she was just suffering last-minute jitters—and the wedding went on. The marriage, however, didn't survive the honeymoon.

Nora was right. If she had known *Nora* better, she would have recognized her misgivings long before she reached the back of church in her wedding gown; she could have acknowledged and expressed her feelings to her partner; she could have called off the engagement before the sense of "too late" became a threat. With a great sense of self-awareness, Nora could have made choices that respected herself and her partner. As it is, her lack of self-understanding led to a great deal of pain for many people.

Religious Convictions

Getting to know yourself includes understanding your personal religious convictions, how you live those convictions, and why. If you were baptized as an infant, you don't remember that your family and friends renounced evil in the world and affirmed their faith in the living God. You don't remember that the water of baptism was poured over you as a sign of your being incorporated into Jesus Christ. You do remember your confirmation, when you were sealed with the Gift of the Holy Spirit. You probably remember your first Communion, when you were taught that Jesus is present in the Eucharist. Your Christian initiation through these sacraments—baptism, confirmation, and Eucharist—gave you an identity as a Christian. With that identity, you have become an adult Christian.

The demands of Christian matrimony can only be understood in light of what it means to be an adult Christian. As a married Christian, your task will be to live your union in the building of a Christian household; your engagement period lays the foundation for that household. As a married Christian, you will strive to live according to Christian principles derived from the Good News that Jesus Christ proclaimed and the Church continues to teach; your engagement period paves the way for that lifestyle. As a married Christian, you will observe the rhythms of the Church year, which serve to anchor your faith; your engagement period tunes your heart to those rhythms. And they will know you are Christians by your love.

Working toward achieving this oneness makes your marriage indissoluble. It is not that you totally achieve one-ness with your beloved, but you experience a oneness even as you experience an incompleteness. Now, during your engaged relationship—which is not indissoluble—you experience feel-ings of both union and distance. This dichotomy makes your engagement an excellent time to examine your religious con-victions.

Whether you are an interreligious couple, a devout or spiritually casual couple, a religiously active or passive couple, you cannot underestimate the influence of your religious convictions. Your engagement provides the time for you to examine your respective convictions to determine how they will affect your lifelong commitment.

What is your conviction about marriage? Jesus' teaching about marriage emphasizes the ancient Genesis reference about the two becoming one flesh (Mark 10:8). As a consequence of their unity of body, mind, and soul in marriage, the couple's union is regarded as indissoluble. Jesus says, "What God has joined together, let no one put asunder" (Mark 10:9). Are you convinced that marriage is meant to be permanent?

Your religious convictions define your behavior as an engaged person. Have you been successful in rejecting those behaviors that attack your relationship? Have you betrayed your partner through infidelity? Have you neglected your partner through lack of attention to and consideration for his or her needs? Have you attempted to dominate or manipulate your partner with various power plays? These behaviors are not aligned with the Christian understanding of marriage.

Has your relationship made you more aware of the beauty of God's creation? Do you live your life according to the gospel principles of love for everyone, especially the needy? Do you see yourself as an agent of reconciliation in the world? How do you put this into practice? Do you seek to know God's will in your daily life? Have you prayed about your engagement? Do you observe Christmas and Easter as more than secular holidays? Reflecting on these questions will help you see how operative your religious convictions already are in your relationship.

Keep in mind that your reflections are not supposed to net final answers. Rather, as you continue to grow, as you learn more about yourself, your beloved, and your relationship, your answers to these questions will shift.

In one of the closing scenes of the movie *Avalon*, the main character is visited in a nursing home by his grandson and great-grandson. He explains to them that he recently visited the old neighborhood. Complaining how it had changed, he says, "Had I known it wouldn't be there, I would have remembered it better." Perhaps, if all of us could remember the significant times and places of our lives, the task of getting to know ourselves could be made easier. Unless you know yourself as well as is humanly possible and unless you can accept yourself with your strengths and failings, you cannot hope to know another—not to the depths that marriage requires. If, however, you have come to know yourself honestly and to accept yourself humbly, you are ready to reflect on getting to know another person.

Reflecting Together

Make a list of any stumbling blocks you've realized in the process of self-examination; invite your beloved to do the same. Exchange your lists and share your insights. Understand that where each of you are now is the result of a great many influences.

Which of these stumbling blocks have caused stress in your relationship?

Consider the driving forces in your life. Do you use them positively or negatively?

Make a list of traits that you like about yourself; make a list of traits about yourself that you don't like. Invite your beloved to do the same. Exchange lists and share your insights. Discuss how these traits have challenged your relationship; how they have enriched your relationship.

Chapter 4

GETTING TO KNOW YOU

*n*ow that you have gained some insight into what makes *you* and what motivates your behavior, it's time to think about what it means to know another person, especially if that person is someone you want to spend your life with. When marriages were arranged by families, a "getting fully acquainted" phase merited little attention. But your love for each other is voluntary; there are no social or familial pressures coercing you to marry. With that freedom, you have the time and luxury of getting to know each other as best you can prior to marriage.

In learning more about each other, you learn more about yourselves, your motivations, your convictions, your strengths, your weaknesses. Some people enter into engagement after a courtship that has let them know each other very well. These couples are ready and eager to marry—and for all the right reasons. Many couples, however, consciously or unconsciously, don't give sufficient attention to the character, actions, and viewpoints of the person they "court." They simply reach a "marrying" age and are willing to marry anyone who's willing. Some persons fear being "passed over" if they don't marry this particular person right now; another chance may not come.

Even if your courtship has been long and you know each other well, your engagement provides a unique stretch of time when marriage is the focus, when you carry in your hearts the very real possibility that "We will spend the rest of our lives together." It is not too late to discover more free and mature reasons for marrying.

If you thought getting to know *you* was difficult, brace yourself: getting to know each other is even more complex. Although you may "read" each other well, you may actually know very little about each other's background and how that impacts the way you relate.

Role Modeling and Your Relationship

Children learn behavior from the behavior their parents model for them. While they learn from both parents, a boy typically learns about being male from his father, and a girl learns about being female from her mother. Overall, children learn about family in this same environment.

Throughout your individual childhoods, role modeling helped each of you develop many positive behaviors: how to be understanding, considerate, and sensitive to peers, loved ones, and those in need. Negative behaviors are usually part of this role modeling as well: how to get your own way and how to dominate others, for example. You also developed certain details about grooming, hygiene, table manners, and social etiquette in this same manner.

Reflecting on what each of you experienced while growing up will help you see why you think and behave in certain ways. If one of your parents tolerated negative behavior from an abusive spouse or simply made no demands in the marriage, you may be timid in being assertive. If one of your parents overlooked inconsiderate behavior or lack of warmth from an indifferent and uninvested spouse, your expectations in marriage may be low—and you may not even be aware of it.

For these reasons, your respective families are not incidental to your relationship. Observe each other's family. Do you see each other model some of the convictions and habits of the family? How might these convictions and habits affect your life over the years? If one of you came from a family that gathers for a formal Sunday dinner every week, and the other came from a family that prefers to drop a waffle into the toaster while taking a break from the crossword puzzle in the morning paper, so what? Well, maybe it's not important—and maybe it is. Your habits somehow reflect how Sunday was celebrated in your respective childhoods.

Of course, we are not suggesting that you scrutinize each other's family. Rather, consider the adage, "The apple doesn't fall far from the tree." You will understand something about the behavior of another person if you know the kind of role modeling given that person in his or her formative years. This is not meant to be an exercise in putting your families in the hot seat. Rather, looking at each other's family helps the two of you see how your attitudes, actions, and patterns have been influenced by the significant persons in your lives—and to compare the differences. Your intention is to find those areas of difference and decide if one or both of you need to change.

Are You Prepared for Change?

Human personality is a dynamic entity. People change emotionally, physically, socially, intellectually, and spiritually. A sad scene for a counselor is that of a teary-eyed spouse who says, "I never suspected that he would ever do that" or "I thought that she was different." How is it that a spouse's behavior can be so surprising? One possibility is poor preparation; the distressing behavior was present all along, it simply wasn't noticed for whatever reason. A second possibility is that, in fact, the behavior is new: somehow, the partner changed.

Before marriage, Amy denied that Will had any faults; in particular, she overlooked his excessive drinking. After marriage, Amy's coping with Will's very real faults, which began to affect their lives on a daily basis, made denial impossible. When she began to point out these concerns to Will, marital stress and conflict followed. Had Will and Amy confronted these shortcomings during their courtship or engagement, they might never have gotten married. Now, struggling to keep what has become a burdensome marriage together, they wonder if it can be saved.

The following scenarios demonstrate some of the hidden concerns that couples can overlook during courtship and engagement:

> Brad, although he was excited about being a father, finds that he resents the time and attention his wife devotes to their children. He's jealous of his children.

Trish always wanted to be a mother, but the reality of motherhood is proving to be far more demanding than she had anticipated. She resents not having time for herself; she resents the endless and thankless chores.

Before Leon married Crystal, he thought her attentions to her mother were signs of healthy mother/daughter relating. Actually, Crystal is dependent on her mother for emotional security.

Kirk was used to spending most of his earnings on himself: sports equipment, clothes, music, personal entertainment. Now, as a husband, he finds that the household budget simply doesn't allow him the total financial freedom he once enjoyed.

Change in you and in your relationship is inevitable. Recognizing the fact that change is a natural part of intimate relating and accepting the challenges of change are two of the key tasks of marriage. When both of you can accept change—in yourselves and in your relationship—and remain very much in love, you have overcome a great hurdle. But, if either of you resents change—in each other or in your relationship—then your union will be in serious trouble.

Unfortunately, you cannot predict the course of events your lives will take. Nor can you say with any degree of certainty that your reactions to what life brings will always be positive. Rather than being discouraged by this great field of unknowns, exercise the faith you have in each other, in your relationship, and in your God. Enter the unknown as an adventure that only the two of you have been blessed to make.

"Blind spots" can be a major complication in the process of change. Blind spots are the behaviors you notice in each other that are disconcerting or disturbing, but are not recognized or acknowledged. At times, blind spots can become so painful that they actually threaten the relationship. Good. Blind spots add to your self-knowledge, and they clarify what you expect of each other.

If you learn to live with and willingly accept each other's behavior, then continuing your relationship is justified. But, don't fool yourselves about this. If you haven't really accepted each other's behavior—if you're harboring the idea that "things will change after we get married" or "that particular behavior isn't really that annoying"—your annoyance will probably blossom again. As painful as it is, respect yourselves and your relationship enough to look at behaviors that are disturbing. Is one of you willing to change? Is one of you willing to accept the behavior? Is the relationship threatened by the behavior?

While you consider the negative impact of change now in order to avoid its ill effects later, it's important to consider the positive challenges of change as well. Change is often the gateway to emotional and intellectual growth. Seek out these opportunities. What can the two of you do together that will expose difficult areas? Spend time with each other's families? attend workshops and seminars? take a course? work on a common project? As you interact in situations that are not routine, you have the opportunity to see where you are different as well as alike. With that insight, you're ready to talk about change.

What Attracted You to Each Other?

The late philosopher, Dietrich von Hildebrand, wrote that the first attraction to a person in a meaningful and lasting relationship is intellectual and that sex and other things flow from that union as if they were added blessings. Most people today would scoff at that idea; in our contemporary society, physical attraction comes first. In fact, sexual experiences often precede getting to know the other person.

Advertisers use sex to sell cars, beer, clothing—anything marketable. Using people as commodities has become common-place. The fact is, however, that premature sex does not strengthen or enrich a relationship. Sex too early in a relationship with no long-term commitment or no depth of emotion ruins more relationships than it nurtures. Research indicates that the earlier a person becomes sexually active, the more likely that person is to continue sexual activity with a variety of persons throughout life. What does this say about that person's ability to be faithful to one partner in the experience of marriage? Think about it; talk about it.

When the decision to become engaged is based merely on physical attraction, the foundation of that marriage is resting on sand. Physical attraction seldom lasts; illness, age, eating and hygiene habits, and any number of other variables eventually affect physical appearances. The hourglass figure gets redistrib-uted; the muscled torso turns to flab. Nothing physical remains the same; sooner or later gravity and time win out.

So what attracts you to each other? What has made the two of you decide that you can be lifelong partners? What are the characteristics that you see in each other that draw you together? Is it more than looks? If you examine all your beloved's positive aspects, what do you see? A winning smile? nice hair? something deeper? How about gentleness? good judgment? a sense of humor? friendliness? generosity? patience? compassion? trustworthiness? loyalty? Do you see any of these?

The list of beautiful aspects is not exhaustive nor will everyone have this particular mix of qualities. If these qualities and others have attracted you to each other, you are building a solid foundation for your marriage. Indeed, facial beauty is only skin deep, but beauty of character is deep within a person. Identify and appreciate these deep qualities you recognize in each other; see them as precious gifts that each of you has been blessed with. Find ways to show your mutual esteem for these qualities.

Mutuality and Equality

The goals of marriage are mutuality and equality. Years ago, these goals did not play a major role in a lifelong relationship; today they do.

Mutuality and equality: what does this mean in a lifelong, intimate relationship? Mutuality and equality puts both persons in the relationship on the same "level." Each partner has the same rights and privileges, the same measure of responsibility and accountability. The man is not "over" the woman; the woman is not "subject" to the man. Traditional roles from previous generations, which served society well, no longer offer the structure that is needed for a healthy and enduring relationship today.

Mutuality and equality in engagement and marriage rejects the notion that your gender alone determines your qualifications of privilege or responsibility. One has no privileges over the other. What is good for one is good for the other; what is expected of one is expected of the other. The fact that previous generations settled for spouses who complemented the other isn't enough today.

There is no middle ground here; there is no room for compromise. You cannot enter into the long-term relationship that marriage demands if you are unwilling to accept each other as equals. This does not mean that the two of you have identical talents, interests, and strengths; you remain two unique human beings. One of you may be brighter, wittier, and more educated;

one of you may be more physically attractive, more sensitive, more caring. These differences do not give you "rights" that the other doesn't have; these differences do not mean that one of you is a better person. Rather, your individual and unique characteristics supplement each other's.

While Lucinda and Larry were engaged, Lucinda got a scholarship to a midwestern university. Larry, who had graduated two years earlier, quit his job on the East Coast. Both of them went to the Midwest to find a place to live and a job for Larry so that Lucinda could take advantage of her scholarship after they were married. The couple married; today, Lucinda studies and teaches at the university while Larry works at Sears. Lucinda's pursuit of her career is as important as Larry's efforts in making a living. If Larry earns less than Lucinda or has a less prestigious position at work, his contributions are by no means "demeaned" because they register as "less"; each contributes an equally vital measure of support to the relationship.

The idea of mutuality and equality carries over into the area of leisure-time activities. If both of you have common interests, great! If you have different interests, great! When you share common interests, your intimacy is enriched; when you share different interests, you discover fresh areas of intimacy that may otherwise go unnoticed.

Chapter Three focused on the value of your personal identity; you were encouraged to recognize differences in your-selves and to accept them, without attempting to place a higher value on one trait to the diminution of another. The same dynamic holds true in your relationship. Difference does not imply better or worse; superior or inferior. Rather, it simply means dissimilarity.

Trust is the soil in which mutuality and equality will thrive. If you are giving, caring, and unselfish with regard to others, you probably expect those virtues to be evident in your relationship. If you grew up in a nurturing environment, you will want to establish your marriage in a nurturing environment. If, however, you were not raised in similar environments, then being nurturing is probably something you don't appreciate. What you really want, and this may be at an unconscious level, is to be treated considerately by each other, to be mutually concerned about physical health and emotional well-being. This includes sexual fulfillment, sensitivity to what is stressful, and a respect for your respective hopes and dreams. Trust is the bedrock in which this mutuality and equality will be cultivated.

Without trust, interpersonal relationships fall apart. Whether it be the trust a parent places in a child, a child places in a parent, a teacher in a student, or a student in a teacher, trust is the virtue that makes an interpersonal relationship firm. If you don't trust each other, beware. If every reason for lateness is treated with suspicion, if every outgoing call is a threat, if secrecy shrouds your history, there can be no lasting, mutually satisfying and qualitative marriage. If lies and deception are any part of your courtship and engagement, already your mutuality and equality are under brutal attack.

Mutuality and equality are difficult for couples to establish; our culture simply does not reinforce behavior that models and supports this kind of justice and respect. Things like looks, education, race, income, and whom you associate with often afforded a person a certain privileged status. In the roots of your relationship, however, mutuality and equality are fundamental.

Ethnic and/or Racial Differences

Ethnicity does not simply refer to your genealogy. Rather, ethnic and racial differences refer to distinct variations in the way you express affection, talk to each other, and interpret human interaction in general—and this is just the tip of the iceberg.

Once outside your own ethnic groups, you may be surprised to discover what a hold your own ethnicity has over you. For example, in your own ethnic environment, you can act within certain parameters that are fairly predictable. Once outside your ethnicity, however, you discover—perhaps with some difficulty—that other parameters exist that don't align with, or even respect, your ethnicity. In one family, for example, spirited discussions and interrupting one another may be a sign of interest—even affection. In another family, however, such behavior is considered rude and uncaring.

Lydia couldn't understand why Gary was so easily insulted. She tried to affirm Gary frequently, but he seemed unusually touchy, especially in social gatherings. When Gary would tell Lydia his version of a conversation with mutual friends, Lydia would be totally surprised; she had heard the conversation in an altogether different way.

One day in her anthropology class, Lydia learned that persons in some cultures receive their identity from the people they are talking with. As the teacher explained this concept, Lydia realized a truth about Gary's nature: he is most comfortable with people who agree with his point of view, who share his general outlook on life. This kind of commonality makes Gary feel affirmed and secure. When he is in a group where disagreement and contention are part of the exchange, Gary feels his identity attacked.

Lydia also learned something about herself. She had assumed that her own nonthreatened personality was the norm. She grew up in a community that prized independence and individualism. Gary grew up in a community that prized group identity. Lydia could care less whether someone agrees with her.

She knows where she stands. But for Gary, agreement is extremely important; it tells him who he is.

Fortunately, our world is becoming more aware of ethnic and racial differences; appreciation for rich cultural diversity is on the rise. This suggests some guidelines for getting along with each other if you are in an interracial or interethnic relationship. For example, don't play the cultural superiority game. Learn to appreciate values in both groups. Realize that some things that bother you may be things that can't change because they are culturally rooted. This could lead to a greater tolerance and less desire to change each other to conform to a common norm.

In the scenario above, Lydia realized that she needed to hear Gary's comments with a loving consideration of his cultural heritage. Lydia no longer contradicts Gary or accuses him of being hypersensitive. Naturally, Gary appreciates this new sensitivity on Lydia's part, and their relationship has deepened.

If you are in an intercultural relationship, appreciate the fact that your relationship is going to be significantly impacted by your respective cultural histories. The more you are under stress in your relationship, the more the cultural differences between you loom large. What's more, they cannot be wiped out. If you trivialize or rationalize your cultural backgrounds, the strength of your relationship is seriously at risk.

Religious Differences

Many couples have no religious differences. It does happen, however, that even in same-faith relationships one person observes religious customs more (or differently) than the other. This is not an insignificant difference. It requires discussion, questioning, and honest dialogue.

Since 1985, the rates of intermarriage among Jews has increased fifty-two percent. A recent report on the rate for Catholic intermarriage puts the figure at forty percent. As a result, some couples worry that their respective religious authorities will "make trouble" for them because they're marrying outside their own group.

Although this is a valid concern, it is a fear that has to be tested; it isn't wise to make decisions based on fear. Rather, find out the facts. For example, the Catholic Church is much more welcoming of interreligious marriages today than it was some decades ago.

For most people who seek a church wedding, religion is important. They are not getting married in a church simply because it's a nice setting or that's the way Mother wants it done. Rather, most couples choose a church wedding because their faith bears on their major life choices.

Now, during your engagement period, learn about each other's religious traditions. What has faith meant in your respective lives? What are the strengths of your respective faiths? What are your respective traditions going to say to you about your marrying an outsider and what practical effects will this have on the celebration of your wedding?

The Catholic party will be told that a permission or a dispensation will be required to marry a non-Catholic. Forms are readily available, and your parish priest will assist you in completing them.

The canon law of the Catholic Church requires that the Catholic partner promise to do everything in his or her power to share the Catholic faith with the children of the marriage, to have them baptized, and to raise them as Catholics. The Catholic is required to inform his or her partner about this promise. You will want to discuss why the Church requires this promise and how it applies to your unique situation.

Here is a perfect opportunity to examine your respective faith traditions, to ask questions about why you do what you do as a member of your faith community, and how the differences in your faith traditions will enrich and challenge—or burden and threaten—your relationship. At this stage, you are primarily trying to understand each other's religious convictions and why you hold them. To guide you through this exploration, you may want to take some of the general principles used in ecumenical and interreligious dialogue: listen to each other with interest; respect rather than refute each other's positions and perspectives; emphasize your points of agreement and celebrate your differences as opportunities for spiritual growth.

The typical dimensions of all religious traditions—and therefore the details you will want to examine—have to do with official teachings, rituals, ethical codes, and Scriptures. Social characteristics are also important, such as the way the religion is organized and the typical external marks associated with the religion, like dress or gestures.

This is a wonderful opportunity for the two of you to grow in appreciation for the differences that sustain each of your religious traditions. Particularly exciting will be the many similarities you actually share. Where possible, attend each other's religious services—not for comparison but for appreciation. How does this particular faith tradition form the person into a better human being by instilling and nurturing values and providing opportunities for religious experiences that truly lead to the heart and mystery of Truth?

Throughout this process, keep in mind that the quality of your communication with each other is going to carry your relationship. Respect and affirmation will go a long way toward leading you to make the right decisions in your interreligious marriage.

Children

This is a broad and crucial topic: What are your respective desires for children? What place will they have in your married life? A self-seeking, pleasure-seeking culture exhibits an antichildren bias; have you noticed? Culturally, children are presented as burdens, troubles to avoid. "Work several years before you have children. Save your money." "Get settled first before you have children." "Don't have kids until you have several years just for yourselves; enjoy yourselves." This "worldly wisdom" makes children "public enemy number one" before they're even conceived. It is family planning taken to its extreme. Too often, couples wait until things are "just right," only to find that the years have narrowed their hearts; they're no longer able to welcome children into their lives. No one disputes the basic fact that you can't have children and everything else. But is a raise, a new living-room set, or a large home more important than a child? On the other hand, of course, it can't be taken for granted that couples intend to have children right away.

If you have serious disagreements about when to have children and how to parent, don't marry! From the outset, you place your relationship in serious jeopardy. To think that you can "work this out" after you're married is to deceive yourselves about the meaning of what marriage is all about. You put yourselves into a situation that can lead to deception, severe disappointments, and endless arguing.

It is not enough, however, to merely talk about having children. Observe how each of you reacts to children. How do you treat your nieces and nephews? children in the neighborhood? children of friends? How do you feel about these children? Some people are good with kids; others think of children as little adults.

Some have a high tolerance for playfulness and spontaneity—common characteristics of childhood. Others have little patience for anything childlike. After watching yourselves, discuss what you've observed. Express your hopes and fears. How can you be supportive of each other's concerns? How can you begin now to prepare your hearts to welcome children and to build healthy parenting skills?

Communication

Couples in marriage counseling often place blame for their problems on a "lack of communication." What they really mean is that they do not speak to each other in meaningful, respectful, loving ways. They are, in fact, communicating; they're simply communicating negative messages.

What is communication like between you? What is the level of communication? the tone? Do certain topics create a tense air between you? Are certain topics "off limits"? Is silence (the "cold shoulder"), anger, fear, or impatience the response to certain topics? If one of you switches to another topic each time plans for the weekend come up, communication has, in fact, taken place. It's verbal, but the evasiveness signals disagreement.

To improve your communication skills, learn to read each other's language of behavior, *verbal* and *nonverbal*. Sometimes, for example, the words one uses in a particular exchange mean just the opposite of what they objectively mean. Have you ever felt lousy but responded chipper and fine when a friend asked, "How's it going?" A sensitive friend will pick up on this and will give you a chance to talk. That kind of sensitivity will lend quality to your level of communication. By the same token, an honest answer in the first place respects the relationship to its fullest.

Verbal communication: Just as loneliness is more than being alone, communication is more than talking. Listening is a vital component of communication. Sharing your thoughts, feelings, or concerns with someone who is present in body only (his or her mind being preoccupied with other things) is a painful and isolating experience.

Carl and Lauren are driving to a friend's house; the radio is on. Lauren begins telling Carl about some of her frustrations at work, but Carl is concentrating on the radio program; he doesn't hear what Lauren is saying. Insensitivity? Perhaps. Rude? Perhaps. Most likely, however, there is simply a conflict in perspectives between Carl and Lauren. Carl turns on the radio to listen to it; Lauren considers the radio as "background atmosphere." Lauren complains that Carl is not listening, when in fact, Carl *is* listening; he's listening to the radio. Carl complains that Lauren won't keep quiet and let him listen to the radio. What's the best solution? Should Carl turn the radio off and listen to Lauren? Should Lauren listen to the radio with Carl? Should Lauren turn the radio off and demand Carl's attention? Should Carl pretend he's listening to Lauren and offer an occasional nod of the head from time to time?

You decide—but remember: when one of you complains that the other is not listening, you're really asking to be included in the intimate part of your lover's life. If you're sensitive to each other, you will pick up this emotional need and respond with attention, not a rational "solution." You will respond with your hearts, not your heads.

Perhaps one of you prefers to avoid serious conversation, lest some past problem surfaces—again. This kind of censorship often occurs when you've failed to forgive, when some past hurt has been left unaddressed and unresolved. While no two people have the same time frame for the healing of wounds, overtures toward forgiveness should always be encouraged. Perhaps a case can be made for "I'll forgive, but I won't forget." But the saying "Forgive and forget" is much more appropriate for lovers; "I won't keep dragging up past wounds every time we have a disagreement."

Keeping the channels of communication open between you means expressing yourselves and being mutually attentive. When you can talk with each other on any topic without battle lines being drawn, you have developed a crucial aspect of a sound interpersonal relationship. There is more to communication than mere conversation. Understand the message you are sending, what you intend to communicate, and the emotional import of the message. Be aware of how the message is received and interpreted. As lovers, the two of you will be direct while being sensitive, confrontational while being gentle, and physically *and* emotionally present.

Conversation is more than waiting your turn to speak. It requires listening to what is being said, attempting to decode the message, and then preparing to reply in an appropriate manner. The two of you will communicate more completely when these conditions are present. Communication in engagement, as in other aspects of life, requires recognizing your mutual rights and unique abilities. Being more articulate, for example, does not translate into "smarter." The less articulate person has much to contribute to an intimate relationship. Such narrow labeling will limit your ability to communicate—which weakens your relationship.

Conversation also requires the refining of listening skills. No matter what is being communicated, the effectiveness of that communication depends on the fact that someone is listening. Listen attentively to fully understand the messages each of you intend to communicate.

Nonverbal communication: Nonverbal communication is very important to your relationship. A tender touch, a warm embrace, an affirming pat on the shoulder, are ways of saying that you enjoy being close, that you value each other, that you're really together in the moment, regardless of how difficult the conversation may be. A tense body, a facial expression, a way of walking or sitting: these forms of communication deliver a message without a word being spoken. All together, these forms of nonverbal communication deepen and clarify the spoken word. Paying attention to both verbal and nonverbal messages takes your communication beyond the surface and into the depths of what is being expressed.

"What Have I Learned?"

Your journey of self-evaluation began with Chapter Three where we asked you to take a good look at your individual selves. If you followed the steps laid out there, you took a good hard look at yourselves as individuals, which prepared you to learn more about each other. Perhaps you found yourselves overwhelmed, feeling like there were more problems than solutions. Sometimes life appears that way. But problems are only a small part of the experience of life. Overall, life—a life of mutuality, love, and respect—offers each of you a treasure chest of wonder and awe.

Along this engagement journey, share the self-knowledge you gain: your hopes, fears, aspirations, drives, dreams, and priorities. This is the work of self-revelation that is so important to a successful union. Your knowledge of yourselves gains even more significance when it is coupled with what you learn about others. You know what you expect from other people, you know what sacrifices you are willing to make for others, and you know the limits of tolerance you have for others.

Ask yourselves, "What have I learned? What have we learned?" Be honest. Perhaps you've learned more about what it takes to be a lifelong partner. Perhaps you've learned more about your own individual gifts and limits. Perhaps you've realized that you need more time to create a Christian engagement that will lead to the lasting marriage you both long for. Perhaps you've realized some major, and potentially destructive, issues that leave you uncertain about building a life together. Regardless of what you've learned, your engagement period is a success as long as you do learn.

If, at this point, you are more certain than ever about your engagement, then your ability to know yourselves and to get to know others will make for a successful journey on the way to your wedding. Your wedding, however, is not the "happy-ever-after" end of the story so often depicted in movie scripts. Rather, your marriage rite is the commencement of a new and richer life, a life that requires faith in each other, faith in your bond, and faith in God. Adequately established, this faith is the wellspring from which your marriage will bear much fruit.

Your journey will take you down unfamiliar paths and surprising detours, but, having lived your engagement period as a solid preparation for marriage, you are well equipped to help make that journey most fulfilling and exciting.

Reflecting Together

What have you learned about each other from discussing the questions from the last chapter? Were there any surprises? How did you deal with those surprises? Were you pleased or distressed with those surprises?

What is your relationship like right now? Are you both satisfied with that? If not, what needs to be discussed and/or changed? Is your relationship more sound or do doubts trouble you? Discuss what you can accept in each other's behavior and what behaviors may cause difficulties.

REFLECTING ON YOUR INTIMACY AND SEXUALITY

uring your engagement period, your sexuality sets tasks for you: to deepen and develop the intimacy that will form the basis of your marriage. During this time, you have a heightened sense of your sexual selves; you feel good about yourselves and you enjoy the physical dimensions of your relationship.

For these reasons, understanding your sexuality is crucial. Because you are embodied selves, your sexuality is a basic dimension of your personhood, which contributes to the unique way you are a man or a woman, which in turn draws you to each other as life partners. Through your sexuality, you communicate with each other and enter into the intimacy called, fittingly, communion with another.

Your Maleness and Femaleness

As you reveal to each other more and more about your masculinity and femininity, you are going to discover what it means to be a man or a woman and how this influences the way you experience the world. Everything you do is done as sexual beings. Your maleness, instinctual and learned, wants most of all—but not exclusively—to control, to achieve, to solve problems, and to bring everything within reason. Your femaleness, instinctual and learned, wants most of all—but not exclusively—to nourish, to care for, to relate, and to settle down.

You will see these aspects of your sexuality coming into play as you tackle the tasks of preparing for your wedding day. These aspects will account for the different approaches you take to completing these tasks and for some of the difficulties you experience in your interpersonal relationships through the years.

While you are engaged, you are learning what it means to be a woman and what it means to be a man. Accepting your own sexuality means you are content—even delight—in each other's sexuality. Since both of you experience the world through your sexuality, insight into each other's experience enlarges the understanding you have of yourselves. Your femininity is complemented by his masculinity. Your masculinity is complemented by her femininity. You come to appreciate this human complementarity all the more when you are in love.

As you gain insights into the roles you've each taken on in life, think about how these roles will apply to your marriage. As always, your individual childhood histories will influence the way you think about this. For example, what unspoken norms in your respective childhoods indicated masculine and feminine chores, masculine and feminine behavior, masculine and feminine emotions?

Nick wanted a traditional marriage. He came from a strong ethnic enclave where the women stayed home and the men went to work. Then, he met Camilla, who outshone him in everything. Nick realized that the marriage he wanted could not be possible with Camilla as a life partner; she simply did not meet the definition of femininity that Nick embraced. Here was the most attractive woman Nick had ever met, and she was off-limits to him as a wife. Yet, Camilla was attracted to Nick's gentlemanly ways. She saw a tenderness in him that others seemed to lack. This couple will have a great deal of work ahead of them, should they become engaged.

As you discuss the details of your wedding day, you will get sharp glimpses of how your respective sexuality influences your likes and dislikes, your needs and preferences, your thoughts and emotions. Let these glimpses lead you to ask questions and dig for details: "Why do I want a large wedding?" "Why do you want your grandmother to be a major part of the service?" "Why do I want an evening wedding instead of an early afternoon one?" "Why do you let your cousin have such an influence on the way you want things?"

Intimacy as the Language of Sexuality

One of the most exciting dimensions of your engagement is the ever-deepening intimacy you experience. Because sexuality is your way of being in the world, it is the entire array of your qualities that constitutes your sexual attractiveness. Because your greatest desire during this time is to learn about each other, and to be totally accepted as individuals, your efforts at closeness are concentrated. It is precisely this need that has brought you together. Maybe, like many of us, you would simply sum it up by saying, "I want to love and to be loved." But what does this mean and what part does intimacy play?

Intimacy maintains your attraction to each other. But intimacy is not some private part of a relationship that is relegated to bedrooms and privacy. To love, to be intimate, includes some of the following attributes:

- You feel like this person understands you.
- You don't have to keep explaining yourself.
- You are able to be yourself and not wear any masks.
- You feel totally at home with this person.
- You get support from this person when you need it.
- You feel especially valued by this person.
- You trust this person.
- You like talking to this person.
- You affirm this person and feel affirmed in return.

To be intimate is to be with each other in situations where you promote each other's welfare, show esteem for each other, give and get emotional support from each other. You understand each other and experience happiness in your relationship.

This is quite a list, hardly exhaustive, and you shouldn't take it for granted. While all these attributes are found in intimate relationships, they are not necessarily found in all of them. To anchor these characteristics in practical realities, ask yourselves, "How do these characteristics apply to our relationship?" Pinpointing these realities allows you to communicate on a level that is both deeply intimate and practical. The end result is a safe place where you both experience comfortable self-disclosure.

Getting to know each other before marriage, crucial to a sound and lasting marriage, is not the accomplishment of a couple of weeks. There are places that create an artificial environment of intimacy, where things get "speeded up." One such place is aboard a ship.

When Polly waved good-bye to her friends at the pier, she seemed genuinely distraught. Later that night, however, on the ship's dance floor in the arms of Kiernan, Polly appeared to be the happiest person alive. During the days that followed, she and Kiernan were engaged in endless conversations, and by the end of the trip, the couple was convinced that they should be together. They married two weeks later.

The marriage lasted one month. Too much of their past had been left out of their conversations. When they no longer had their meals served and their cabins cleaned for them, the couple was faced with the harsh realities of everyday life. Their shipboard romance had been a honeymoon before their marriage; they had overlooked engagement altogether.

Your engagement states that you have reached a certain level of intimacy, that you want to deepen your intimacy and make it the basis of your marriage. This expression of your respective sexualities, which is oriented to achieve intimacy, is fundamental to your relationship and serves as the atmosphere in which your total communion is expressed in the act of inter-course.

Intimacy as the Language of Acceptance

During your engagement, you will discover weaknesses and negative characteristics in each other. Through intimacy, you can face these concerns with honesty.

Intimacy allows you to accept your own limitations and each other's. Naturally, you will each try to change what you can. When change is difficult or impossible, however, your intimacy is where you affirm each other, offer acceptance and encouragement, and reassure each other when you fail.

Intimacy, and the role it plays in acceptance, teaches you tolerance. Noticing each other's strong points and, only later, after the relationship deepens, noticing each other's weaknesses, is a normal process. Your respective weaknesses give each of you a realistic perspective and prevent you from loving your own idealization of each other. This is especially clear when one of you has projected an idealized picture onto the other only to find out that the reality is significantly different. The recognition of the difference between your projection and reality is a sign of the maturing of your relationship. The more you accept each other as you really are, the more your energy will be focused on the real needs of your relationship.

Intimacy as the Language of Unity

Your sexuality is not some abstract part of human nature. Rather, it is part of the way you act in the world. Since your sexuality is oriented toward overcoming isolation, it leads you to make the engagement period an exciting and memorable one. All the activities associated with planning the wedding bring you together. You make decisions about wedding and reception music, your wedding and honeymoon clothes, the wedding cake, the flowers, the furniture for your own household, and where you're going to live. In many of these activities, your parents will play a role since a marriage is a family affair.

Gerry and Frances were to be married in five weeks. Frances' mother, however, continued to complicate things. Her disappointment with her own wedding reception thirty years ago made her determined to have things "just right" for her daughter—regardless of what her daughter and future son-in-law wanted. Tension in the family was sharp, making everyone uncomfortable. Frances tried to reason with her mother; Frances' father and fiancé tried to reason with the woman. No one got results.

Claudia and Phil had a different experience. Their parents were respectful of all their wishes in the planning of the wedding. Everything moved by suggestion and discussion. Each discussion began with "Well, what does the bride and groom want?" Claudia and Phil were free to choose, change their minds, and choose again. The process of planning was fun, and the wedding day was memorable.

Both families brought to their decision-making process their habitual ways of acting, which in turn impacted the couple. Because the couple had used their engagement as a time to deepen their intimacy, they were able to understand the power of family influences. They knew that the process of getting married involves many family units, all in the process of creating yet another family unit. Without intimacy, without the depths of respect, sharing, and understanding that intimacy provides, you have no common language with which to communicate.

Intimacy as the Language of Fun

Nothing adds a sweeter ingredient to fun than to be with someone who knows you and invites you into the freedom of play. Make time for fun activities that allow you to strengthen your bond as a couple. Some couples enjoy amusement parks and cultural or sports events. They enjoy the company of other friends—and they enjoy their time alone.

During your engagement, stimulate your relationship with different activities. Enjoy the things you have in common; enjoy the things you don't have in common; enjoy the things that neither of you knows anything about. Your engagement is a wonderful time to exercise your creativity since you are probably in one of the greatest creative moments of your life. Use this time to explore, to find out more about what you enjoy as individuals and as a couple. Often times, couples find that what they didn't like doing alone or with friends they thoroughly enjoy doing with their beloved.

In movies, when couples fall in love, there is usually a series of scenes that shows the lovers walking hand in hand in the park, laughing through city streets, and talking long and deeply over late dinners and early breakfasts. These scenes vividly capture the fun and freedom of the love relationship. They show the many aspects of human sexuality that bring out a lightheartedness. Because your sexuality leads you to overcome the distances that separate you, the fun you enjoy together deepens your intimacy. Your bodies, your emotions, and your selves all come together in the mutual exchange of love while you're at play.

Making the Right Effort

No relationship can survive on automatic pilot; the love you experience interiorly needs to be externalized. Some external expression, of course, is effortless; it comes naturally. Buying gifts for each other, holding hands, touching, and simple courtesies take no effort, no conscious thought.

But a great deal of effort is required in certain areas of your relationship; this is where we draw your attention.

Some situations take just the right effort. While no single example will apply to everyone, the example of attendance at a marriage-preparation program sponsored by the Church is common. Imagine that one of you wants to attend; the other doesn't. Both of you have to put forth a great deal of effort with this difference of opinion, an effort that is directed at the good of your relationship and not at the merits of a local pastoral program. It is an expression of just how intimate you are if you can really listen to each other and appreciate each other's point of view. Mutual understanding and seeking to please each other are signs of your intimacy. When you put the right effort into working at your relationship, even your disagreements can become occasions for achieving intimacy.

Jay was a bachelor. We wondered why he wasn't married. He said that he had been engaged twice. The first time he romanced his sweetheart "with flowers, movies, the whole bit." But she called it off. The second time he got engaged, he decided that he didn't need to go through "the whole romance routine." Jay claimed, "It was a waste of time if we really loved each other." His partner disagreed: she wanted to be romanced. They broke up.

Jay approached engagement as if it were only a question of biding time. He didn't think he had to prove himself by giving his partner extra-special attention. She was supposed to know how much he loved her without his showing it. Jay's way of acting was not much different from Henry Higgins in *My Fair Lady*, who wanted to know, "Why can't a woman be like a man?"

The rituals of courtship and engagement cannot be taken lightly. Your relationship is the most important thing to you right now. If you're truly in love with each other, you do everything in your power to preserve and foster this relationship—and that takes effort!

One survey reported that women formed the majority of those enrolled in college courses dealing with marriage and relationships. It seems that women, more than men, value working at and learning about relationships. In our experience, young women in our courses seem to be much more in tune with the reality of their relationships than the men. If this is generally true, then it may also explain why in another survey males tended to perceive their relationships to be in better shape than their women partners perceived them to be.

Do women expect more out of a relationship than men do? If so, then men must make an effort to see the messages their partners are sending them about this, and women must make their wishes known and not presuppose that men know what they are thinking.

Appreciating each other's uniqueness takes just the right effort. There is a terrible paradox in human relationships; we don't know what we have until we lose it. Your engagement is the time to cultivate the habit of discovering each other's uniqueness. This requires special effort, especially if routine sets in and you begin to take each other for granted. Surprise each other; learn to value each other's attitudes and actions.

Fulfilled human beings can move away from their own self-centeredness to be open to the interior beauty of other persons. This, in fact, is a primary goal of your sexuality, which is oriented toward relating to each other with emotional warmth and compassion. As soon as you think you can "read him (her) like a book," you are closing the chapter on your relationship. It's not that you have no more to offer each other or that you know each other thoroughly; rather you've grown nearsighted and have taken the part for the whole.

Do not mistake the predictable parts of your interaction for the whole of your relationship. When the relationship is in trouble, for example, the right kind of effort is required to lead you to look at the trouble, to see where it came from, and to discover how dealing with the issues enhance your bond.

In this process, be on your guard against certain weaknesses that might prevent your movement toward reconciliation. Don't let past models of behavior or old attitudes hold you back from risking new ways of doing things and looking at things.

Your sexuality plays an important role in these efforts as well. It is in the very nature of your sexuality to seek to communicate and to know communion. You fell in love not by accident but on purpose, as a way of fulfilling your individual human capabilities. Putting effort into reconciling when you have had a falling out is a mark of your maturity in your sexual development.

Be respectful of the different ways men and women have been socialized to deal with fighting and making up. In *You Just Don't Understand: Women and Men in Conversation*, Deborah Tannen makes a plea for flexibility: "Women who avoid conflict at all costs would be better off if they learned that a little conflict won't kill them. And men who habitually take oppositional stances would be better off if they broke their addiction to conflict."

Control of your sexual urges takes just the right effort. Your sexuality includes that biological dimension of your human nature called sex, which is oriented toward procreation and pleasure. In some relationships, however, sex takes on such importance that sexuality is undervalued. Indeed, sexuality may be so undervalued in a relationship that sexual intercourse serves as a substitute for intimacy rather than as its affirmation.

Part of your developmental task is to get control of your genital expression; learn to understand your desires, and learn to control them. Not every desire is to be acted on. In their journey toward mature relationships with the opposite sex, people's sexual desires can often seem overpowering; to think of controlling these desires seems to mock human nature. Yet, education in self-control is important for maturity and for living in society. Sexual self-control is motivated by a respect for each other as persons. Love that is eminently human is love that comes from your desire to seek each other's good, not simply the satisfaction of your own desires.

Your love is a mutual and shared love, not one that attempts to appropriate. This is why control of your sexual impulses must be in the service of a mature, affective, intimate relationship. Even in marriage, this kind of sexual restraint and control, governed by respect for each other, must be present.

Thus, the Church tells cohabiting couples, as part of their marriage preparation, to live apart until their wedding day. This often strikes the cohabiting couple as silly, dishonest, or an interference in their personal decisions. The request, however, is not a manipulating demand. The Catholic Church holds that "sexual intercourse finds its full significance only in marriage." It would be dishonest for the Church to approve sexual activity outside of marriage.

But there's actually more to it than that. When sexual intercourse takes place during engagement on a regular basis, it affects how the couple perceives their relationship. Quite naturally, they think that their sexual intercourse means they should get married. They understand that there is a deep relationship between regular sexual intercourse and commitment. What they may fail to see, and what may be true in some cases, is that regular sexual intercourse during engagement can get in the way of an honest understanding of where the relationship is actually rooted. A couple could easily be led to consider marriage, not because of the depth of their interpersonal relationship, but because of the frequency of their sexual relationship. Abstinence gives the couple a chance to see just what their relationship is based on. If physical relating is the extent of what holds the relationship together, there will be little contentment and genuine commitment for the lifelong adventure of marriage.

Sexuality Moves Toward Union

The natural movement of your sexuality is to seek union, sexual union, with each other. When you fell in love, you found yourselves naturally—and with much satisfaction—affirming each other. In each other and in the relationship you were creating, you found a place where you, as individuals, were accepted, appreciated, and affirmed in just who you are: no artificiality.

Within your relationship, where this acceptance and affirmation is mutual, your sexual attraction to each other finds fulfillment, which ultimately comes to be expressed in sexual intercourse in marriage, an expression that goes beyond the mere satisfaction of your biological instincts. The meaning of your sexual intercourse in marriage is seen more clearly when it is placed in relationship to the mutual consent you exchange on your wedding day. On that day, your verbal consent is sealed by your bodily union. Together these two expressions constitute the initial making of a marriage. In this way, your sexual intercourse becomes a part of the total self-giving you declare on your wedding day. It is not used as a commodity to be exchanged for favors granted; it is not a mechanism used to cope with tension or loneliness. This is what gives special meaning to the words, "I'm saving myself for my future wife" or "I'm saving myself for my future husband."

The quality of your sexual intercourse depends on the kind of people you are. Common sense tells you that a selfish person will be self-seeking in intercourse; an uncaring person will be uncaring in intercourse; a rude person will be rude in intercourse. To ensure that your experience of sexual intercourse will be a celebration of your union, take the time to develop a heightened awareness of each other as persons worthy of love and honor. In exercising all facets of your sexuality and in the context of mutual total self-giving, you prepare for marital sexual intercourse that is happy, fantastic, fun, and a deeply moving experience.

"I will love and honor you all the days of my life" may not correspond to the reality of the true nature of a relationship that is based on mutual sexual attraction. There may be no real intention to be faithful. There may be no real intention to build a lifetime marriage because "great sex" has prevented the couple from really knowing each other. Marriage by mutual sexual attraction that motivates the couple to know each other in the fullest sense of the word, on the other hand, is a marriage that has a rich and lasting future.

Consider how Jesus lived his sexuality. In the gospels, Jesus appears assertive and gentle, a friend of men and of women, an excellent teacher, brave and dignified, a leader and a listener. Both men and women have been attracted to Jesus precisely because of the way he lived his sexuality. Embracing these characteristics in his own life, Jesus related to people with respect, honesty, and consideration. He did not judge; he did not relate to people with a set of rules and expectations. He loved, purely and openly. He enjoyed a good time, with positively no regard for how his social status might appeal to the local community. He loved. How fitting that Jesus often used the image of a bridegroom; he saw himself as introducing a time of newness and joy with his announcement that the kingdom of heaven was at hand. What a perfect analogy for the beginning of your married life!

Jesus shows the way to relate to each other. His focus on others, and on their ultimate good, is a model for your engagement. Use your engagement period to practice love as Jesus loved. Use this time for nongenital expressions of affection, for focusing on each other's total good, for getting to know each other fully. With this kind of intimacy building toward sexual intercourse, your genital expressions of love are far more honest, far more meaningful, and far more celebrative of the union you seek.

Sexuality and the Transmission of Human Life

As your membership in your own family shows, the movement of human sexuality is toward union with another person and toward the procreation and rearing of children. During your engagement, while your sexuality prepares you for union and communion, you are also creating the human environment into which new human life will be welcomed. Your very sexuality shows that you are made for reproducing human life and that your love for each other is a love open to welcoming other persons into it. In this sense, your engagement period is not only important for the two of you but also for those children you will welcome into your marriage. The life that you give each other in your relationship of love has, as its natural goal, the transmission of human life to those who will be your children.

Having children should be no accident. You should eagerly welcome children and provide a sound environment for their secure upbringing. This process and planning cannot be crammed into a nine-month pregnancy. Now, as an engaged couple, you prepare to welcome children.

As part of your preparation for marriage, you will be introduced to natural family planning, a means of planning your family that is based on the natural aspects of your mutual fertility. Because it uses no artificial methods of contraception, natural family planning allows the couple to share in the responsibility of both controlling and avoiding conception. Natural family planning also allows the couple to learn something about their fertility cycles.

Now, during your engagement, consider the many mysterious dimensions of the monthly menstrual cycle; it will be a major part of your sexual expressions throughout your married life. As a woman, you have the unmatched opportunity of sharing a phenomenal part of your personhood with the man you love. As her lover, you, the male, have an unmatched opportunity to learn about an integral dimension of your beloved.

The Sacramentality of Sexuality

The sacramentality of sexuality means that our very human sexuality reveals something about the divine reality we call God. The Catholic Church teaches that God intends for you to find your authentic human beingness in relationship with other persons and in particular with each other in marriage. Just as your sexuality is intrinsic to getting to know each other, it is intrinsic to your relationship with God. In achieving intimate communion with each other, you experience God's commitment to you. By loving each other whom you can see, you show your capacity to love God whom you cannot see.

To contemplate the mystery of your sexuality is to see the wonderful gift that human sexuality is for living a happy satisfying life, for understanding something about the mystery of God, and for entering into a personal relationship with God. With your sexuality, you reach out to each other—and respond to each other. You create, the two of you now and with your children later, a community of persons. Thus, your sexuality becomes for you one of your greatest resources for thinking about the gracious Creator who wishes to overcome all obstacles to a loving relationship.

Engaged love, born of great affection and sexual attraction, prepares you for marital love, which is to increase and deepen through the years what your engagement promises. In living married life, you will discover how your love gets perfected and transformed through the grace of God working through your sexuality.

Toward the Wedding

In the beginning was the relationship. In the biblical story of creation, Adam is created out of the earth before Eve. He finds himself lonely. The creation of the other animals leaves him more lonely, for none of them can be his mate. God puts Adam into a deep sleep and creates Eve from one of his ribs. Adam is ecstatic at the creation of Eve: "This is bone of my bone, flesh of my flesh!" This story shows the unity of Adam and Eve as persons.

Thus, in the biblical account, there is an initial affirmation of our sex and sexuality. But the story does not end there. Man and woman must leave the garden of Eden, at which point, the story makes an important point about our sexuality. Outside the garden, human beings have the developmental task to achieve the integration of their sexuality and their personality.

The biblical account, of course, is a foundational story. There is an original goodness followed by an original expulsion into the world as we know it. Since then, there has been a desire to return to the original unity. The message of Jesus is that the return to the original unity passes by way of love.

God is love. God is the origin and the goal of human love. As creatures of this loving God, in whose image and likeness you are made, your nature is loving, especially designed to love the Creator. In fact, the proof that you love the Creator is that you love each other, God's creations.

Contemporary spirituality, however, sees the love of Christians as something far broader than a couple in love. Christian love is embodied and carried out in concern and care for many others; it pursues justice for everyone; it builds peace. It is a love that is directed toward the wider community.

How do these two powerful loves merge in the life of the Christian? There is no merging; by nature, they are two sides of the same coin. Both loves are personal. Both seek the good of others. Both are a share of one's personhood in a human encounter with another person or persons.

As you love each other during your engagement, you experience a love that is the connecting force of the universe. You love with the love of God, and you love in response to God's invitation to love. The relationship you share, based on love, is the life of your commitment throughout marriage. The love you share today is the bedrock on which you will come to know greater depths and broader vistas of love in the world as a married couple. This love is the beginning of a love that will support and transform both of you as spouses, a love that speaks of God's supporting and transforming love for all humankind.

Already God blesses your love.

Reflecting Together

Reread the list of attributes associated with intimacy on page 72. Would you add more attributes or consider some irrelevant to intimacy? Why?

"Sexual intercourse finds its full significance only in marriage." These words from page 80 go counter to many messages that you receive from popular culture. As you understand more deeply the role that commitment plays in your relationship and as you look forward to the total commitment you will make to each other at your wedding, how do you understand the Church's position on the relationship between sexual intercourse and marriage?

Chapter 6

UNDERSTANDING YOUR ENGAGEMENT SPIRITUALITY

*T*here is a spirituality proper to every stage of our lives. As we advance in age and maturity, and as our life situations shift, the spirituality that helps us live meaningful lives is usually staring us right in the face.

Engagement spirituality is not some added religious dimension that you work into your lives during this time. Rather, engaged spirituality is a composite of attitudes, values, and convictions appropriate to engaged couples. In this sense, the previous chapters have dealt with spirituality. It could not be otherwise, since we are spiritual and material beings at one and the same time.

What are some of the characteristics of engagement spirituality that make your relationship flourish? How does the Catholic sacramental viewpoint give shape to your world view as engaged individuals?

Seeing Beyond the Obvious

Imagine that you're on a crowded bus on a gloomy Monday morning. Everyone headed back to work is in a bad mood. You look up and see a couple full of gaiety and laughter boarding the bus. You're surprised by this moment of goodness. Their light-heartedness, their obvious delight in each other, has affected your own attitude. You feel better about the day.

This analogy, adapted from a poem by Ezra Pound, reveals something of the way Christians think about the world. The lovers' ardent spirit points to the gracious love that is at the heart of the universe. Think of a married couple you like and admire. No doubt, they are just ordinary people. But because they are capable of being bearers of God's love for others, their relationship is a symbol of more than themselves. When they radiate their love for each other and for you, their marriage is a sacrament of God's love for the world.

This way of thinking is rooted in the central Christian teaching called the Incarnation. As Saint John put it, "For God so loved the world that he gave his only Son, that everyone who believes in him may not perish but have eternal life" (3:16). The Nicene Creed, recited at the Sunday Eucharist, says, "He was born of the Virgin Mary, and became man." This is the Incarnation. All those who encountered Jesus, the man from Nazareth, encountered more than just another human being. They encountered the Christ, the Son of God.

This sacramental way of understanding Jesus helps explain how the Church understands its worship. There is always more than meets the eye. At the Eucharist, for example, a prayer of thanksgiving is said over the bread and wine. These simple elements have human and cosmic significance because they are products of both natural elements and human intelligence. They come from seeds planted in the earth, that are matured through the energies of sun, wind, and rain. Through human skill, the wheat and the grapes are made into food and drink. As the prayer at the rite of preparation says, "They are fruit of the earth and the work of human hands."

Bread and wine are for eating and drinking, the two essential activities for human nourishment. Sharing them with others embodies our human community as one, united in the bread and wine. To share food with others is to wish them the prolongation of life. In the Christian context of liturgy and faith, this human meaning of bread and wine is given a deeper meaning. The priest invokes the Holy Spirit upon the bread and wine so that they may be further transformed, that they may become the body and blood of Christ and unite all who participate. The community itself becomes the Body of Christ.

This array of symbolism reveals the true reality of our existence in the world. Through the natural, physical realities of the world, we partake in divine realities. Just as the wheat and the fruit are first transformed into bread and wine and then transformed further into the body and blood of Christ, all Christians are called to be transformed by Christ and the Holy Spirit.

At your wedding liturgy, you will celebrate this same transformation. Your individual lives will be blessed as one life that bears Christ to all. Your individuality is not compromised or lost, but is brought together and transformed through the power of the Holy Spirit as you become more than two separate individuals. Your love for each other reveals, in some way, the mystery of God's love for the world.

Your love for each other during your engagement is a transforming love. For others, your love is a sign of the transforming power at the heart of the universe. Throughout your marriage—and now during your engagement—your love for each other takes flesh in your desire to be a couple. Your engagement and your eventual marriage are an incarnational manifestation.

You are moving toward Christian marriage, which from a sacramental perspective, is the sign and symbol of God's love for creation and Christ's love for the Church. This spiritual orientation is the cornerstone on which your Christian marriage will rest. Does this make you uncomfortable? Does this sound like a lot to expect when so many other areas of life are laced with change and adjustment? It is! The love you have for each other is not yours and yours alone; the love you share is a gift for us all.

Your Marriage as a Sacrament

When the Church refers to your marriage as a sacrament, she is referring to both the celebration of the wedding and the achievement of your marital union. Because most Catholics are baptized as infants, they often think of a sacrament as something "received," something "done to" someone—which is accurate. "Receiving" a sacrament is to receive the goodness of God, to experience God doing something for us through the Christian community to which we belong. When we baptize babies, for example, they become part of a loving community of believers. God gives them, through their faith community, an explicit share in the abundant life that Jesus won for all persons.

To understand what Christian baptism accomplishes from the sacramental viewpoint, consider this remarkable passage from the Letter to the Ephesians (1:4-8). Read it line by line as a piece of poetry, pausing to pay attention to the meaning of each thought.

> *God the Father chose us in Christ*
> *before the foundation of the world*
> *to be holy and blameless before him in love.*
> *God destined us for adoption as his children*
> *through Jesus Christ,*
> *according to the good pleasure of his will,*
> *to the praise of God's glorious grace*
> *that God freely bestowed on us in the Beloved.*
> *In him we have redemption through his blood,*
> *the forgiveness of our trespasses,*
> *according to the riches of God's grace*
> *that God lavished on us.*

This passage reveals how baptism is a Christian sacrament that manifests God's prior love for you, declares it, and makes it actual in you. Note two of the key verbs in the passage: *chose* and *destined*. As an engaged couple, you can resonate with these words because you, too, have experienced yourselves as "chosen" by each other to consider a life that is "destined" to be shared in a lifelong bond. Your very engagement illustrates what the Letter to the Ephesians affirms about the newly baptized.

Your parents, too, actualized God's love for you in a vivid and concrete way. Your parents created an environment for you that made you feel valued and secure. In this environment, they were the first to communicate to you Christian values drawn from the gospel. Thus, if you were baptized as an infant, you were profoundly blessed by God in your family and in the larger faith community to which you and they belonged. Your baptism was a social occasion, but it was also more. It was a religious experience with lasting effects.

In the New Testament, the more common experience of baptism is not infant baptism but the baptism of those who have heard the preaching of the gospel and have assented to it. In these cases, baptism follows conversion. The washing of the converted person symbolically ritualizes the conversion that has already taken place in the heart of the person being baptized, who from now on will live as a Christian. This full, conscious, and active participation in the sacrament of baptism is a celebration of a conversion experience; it shows that baptism is not something that happens to the person. It is an *active* receiving, not a passive one.

Whether you were baptized as an adult, following a time of faith formation, or as an infant, and then raised in a Christian environment, your faith has shaped your identity over the years.

Engagement as a Ritual Part of the Sacrament of Marriage

The path to marriage, and marriage itself, exemplifies this dynamic meaning of a sacrament. Before approaching the Church about marriage, the two of you have been getting to know each other better through dating—and now through your engagement period. You've been sharing joys and sorrows, learning about each other's life histories, delighting in your mutual love. You've been giving others an image of yourself as a couple. While the wedding liturgy will be a public declaration of your consent to take each other in sickness and in health, in good times and in bad, all the days of your lives, it will also be an expression of all that has led up to that public moment. The ritual giving and taking in the sacrament of marriage celebrates your mutual giving and taking that took root and deepened before and during your engagement.

This liturgical moment will not be the first ritual that has marked your journey toward marriage. How you came to be engaged was a very important ritual that initiated this part of your journey. Perhaps it was a simple question: "Will you marry me?" Maybe you took a more elaborate approach, like hiring an airplane to do a sky-written message, or declaring your love and proposal on a billboard. Whatever your style, your decision to get engaged was the movement from one stage of your relationship into another. And you marked this movement with a declaration of intent, between yourselves and eventually to your families and friends. Perhaps you marked it with the giving of an engagement ring or some other significant symbol.

The eventual celebration of your marriage will flow from the dynamic relationship you now enjoy during your engagement period. The ritual of the wedding ceremony itself will be one more in a line of rituals that mark your journey along the path of marriage. The act of engagement celebrated your readiness to move your relationship further along the road; by becoming engaged, you took on the responsibility to begin developing your relationship into a marriage. As an engaged couple today, you are working on your marriage.

Your Marriage Lived as a Sacrament

Just as the sacrament of baptism is lived out in your everyday lives, so the sacrament of marriage is more than the wedding day activities. Rather, the sacrament of marriage is your relationship lived from the viewpoint of Christian faith. It is a way of living your baptism. You become the mirror of God's love, for each other, for your families and friends, and for the children you will someday welcome into your lives.

This understanding of marriage as a sacrament does not neglect your natural human limitations. You will err; all human beings do. But in the context of your marriage as a sacrament, your internalized Christian values guide your efforts to love, to forgive, and to be open to the conversion to which God continually calls you. Your marriage, built on fidelity and mutual respect, will be the place for your triumphs and failures, your joys and your sorrows, your kindness and anger, your terrific communications and your terrible misunderstandings: your life together in good times and in bad.

So the love of a woman for a man, of a man for a woman, of a man and a woman for their children, is meant to be the mirror of God's love. Obviously, this is a calling that demands a great deal from you if it is to be realized; it does not happen automatically or mechanically. Living your marriage as a sacrament means that you take your Christian baptism seriously, that your life of Christian discipleship is rooted in your bond of marriage. Your many acts of love, expressed with tenderness and patience, always concerned for the good of each other, are the signs of God's love. Especially to each other, you are the living symbols of God's love.

In Christian marriage, spiritual, physical, and natural realities intersect and interact in a special way. The sacrament you are called to live is the sacrament you will minister to each other at your wedding ceremony and in your day-to-day lives. The world needs your sacrament; the world needs honeymoon lovers who are ready to risk all for the hope of promise and love. Over the years, as your love matures, your sacrament will change—and the world needs that as well. As you become seasoned lovers, lovers faithful to each other until death, lovers who live the sacrament of marriage, the world glimpses the promise of eternal life.

Engagement Spirituality

You begin this way of living your marriage now, by living it first during your engagement. Engagement spirituality is not a vague and mysterious phenomenon suited for only some "very spiritual" couples. Engagement spirituality is for everyone who loves another person.

Your engagement spirituality is characterized by gratitude. God the Creator has blessed you with each other, and you are drawn into a more intimate relationship with God as a result of that blessed gift. Your engagement spirituality is also characterized by *care, affirmation, love,* and *reaching out.*

Care: Your engagement is spiritual because it is characterized by caring. You have experienced caring before: your parents cared for you, and you cared for your parents. But your engagement experience is an intense caring for another individual outside the family unit. You may have known this caring outside the family in previous relationships, but the experience of caring within the context of engagement is a caring that is directed toward a freely chosen and publicly declared lifelong bond. You are emotionally, spiritually, and physically available to each other, primarily and exclusively. You rejoice with each other's joy; you struggle with each other's concerns. With immediate and total care for the other, you are a couple.

Karen was close to her maternal grandmother. When her grandmother died after a brief illness, Karen felt tremendous grief. She longed to share her grief with her parents, but they were absorbed with funeral arrangements and practical details. Karen's fiancé, Barry, sensed what she was going through; he could see that Karen was hurting and needed someone to hear her pain. Barry adjusted his work schedule to be as available as he could to Karen. This wasn't a burden for Barry or something he felt obligated to do. As a result of his engagement spirituality, his loving care naturally focused on the needs of his beloved.

Care is brought to bear on disagreements as well. Your closeness does not give you a license to treat each other lightly. On the contrary, it leads you to a mutual respect that no issue can undermine. Care, in the midst of disagreements, keeps you from becoming defensive and vindictive. Care allows you to admit faults and insensitivities and softens your hearts to ask for and accept forgiveness.

Theresa had the cruel habit of slapping people when she got angry with them. Naturally, being on her best behavior, she controlled this behavior when she was around Jaime. Shortly after she became engaged to Jaime, however, Theresa lost her temper at something Jaime said. In reflex fashion, she raised her hand to strike Jaime in the face. Jaime grabbed Theresa's arm in midair and told her that he didn't want to be slapped and that if he had said something wrong he was sorry. He firmly told Theresa that slapping was not a behavior he would tolerate and that he would never let her slap him. He did not want their relationship to involve physical assault of any kind.

Theresa had mixed emotions. She was glad that Jaime had stopped her, but Jaime's words were upsetting. She understood that Jaime did not want physical abuse to be part of their relationship but, as she pointed out to Jaime, his words were to her a slap that delivered as much of a sting as skin hitting skin.

Immediately, Jaime realized that Theresa was right. He had inadvertently hurt her deeply. He had spoken his mind, remaining firm in his principles, but he was insensitive to how Theresa received him.

Theresa and Jaime obviously cared for each other on many levels. Because of their deep care for each other, this was an important moment in their relationship. Both discovered a depth of feeling, within themselves and in each other, that would serve their bond in the long haul of day-to-day life.

Caring for others is also part of your engagement spirituality. In your circle of care, you develop a loving concern for each other's families, friends, and coworkers. You care for all those who are important to your shared life. Your circle of friends broadens, your social activities become more varied, and your special-events schedule is arranged to respect both families. When tension develops, as it will, your communication skills and the personal growth that you've both realized throughout your engagement will enable the two of you to respond to each other—and to others—with care.

Especially important in this circle of love are your respective families. Your engagement, while it may cause some stress between family members, is an opportunity for the two of you to come to a greater appreciation of family. In your exchanges with the people who will be your in-laws, both of you have opportunities to build a sense of extended family that will support you through the years. You may see in each other's parents, for example, special qualities that you, as the adult children, have never noticed. Your engagement affords you the time to make these observations, to share them, and to anticipate what being part of family will entail.

The Clarks liked Clara, their son's fiancée. Mark noted Clara's warmth and concern for his parents, and over a short period of time, began to emulate that same warmth and concern. Mark also responded to his parents' acceptance of Clara. He sensed a new identity with his parents; having become part of a couple himself, he was more aware of—and appreciative of—his parents as a couple. As an engaged couple, Mark and Clara were beginning to understand something about their parents that they hadn't realized before. Their parents didn't live independently of each other; their "coupleness" was a major dimension of their lives. After Mark and Clara married, both Mark's and Clara's families admitted that their families were richer because of the "new member" they had gained.

Care is an evident part of your engagement spirituality in the way you care for your own body and each other's. In fact, you're probably more aware of physical well-being, diet, and exercise than you've ever been. You want to be healthy; you want your beloved to be healthy. What and how much you eat and drink, how much exercise you get, whether or not you smoke, and your personal habits of cleanliness are matters that take on a heightened level of attention and concern during your engagement period.

But this is a delicate area. In fact, you may disagree about certain details in this area. When Harry remarked to Marsha that she ate a lot of ice cream, Marsha got upset and said, "Am I that fat?" "I only meant to observe how much ice cream you eat, that's all," Harry explained. But Marsha didn't believe him, and rightly so. Harry was concerned for Marsha; he did not want her weight to become a health hazard. Although the comment was received as a criticism, it was meant to be helpful. Harry might have expressed his concerns in a more delicate manner; he might have suggested that they both begin to exercise together or join the local YMCA.

Perhaps one of you is more in touch with health needs, diets, exercise, and hygiene. Learn to respect and care for that part of your relationship. To be your physical and mental best for each other is part of the way you say "I love you."

Certainly as important—and perhaps more important—is the care for each other's bodies in the sexual domain. Your intimacy arouses deep emotional and physical feelings between you. How you express those emotions and physical feelings during your engagement fashions your expressions of intimacy for years to come.

It isn't unusual for engaged couples to have sex. "We're going to get married; what difference does it make?" is the usual rationale. Or "What difference does it make? We were having sex before we were engaged; why should we stop now that we're planning to be married?" Put in the context of marital spirituality, premarital sex takes on a different perspective.

Certainly, whenever two people make love—when the exchange is mutually caring, tender, and genuinely committed—both are deeply affirmed. Lovemaking deepens your sense of union and offers you an expression of care that is powerfully personal. A caring spirituality during engagement calls for a careful consideration of how you express physical intimacy during this time.

Many couples defend their lovemaking during the engagement period by insisting that if they are both willing, loving, tender, and neither gets hurt, there is nothing inappropriate about the expression. From this perspective, making love is always right, always healthful. Others see lovemaking as a natural by-product of their love; something that they can't control—and shouldn't because they "love" each other and intend to marry.

Consider this, however: sexual intercourse escalates (once is not enough) and involves you at your deepest levels, especially when you love each other and are putting a life together. But lovemaking is not something you "do" like shopping or bill paying. Lovemaking cannot be turned on and off like an appliance; every act affects you. Lovemaking is the crown of your total commitment to each other, a commitment that is not complete without the witness and support of community—which is what your wedding day is all about.

"*Why?*" some of you may ask with insistence and frustration. Why? Because sexual intercourse is a powerful experience, so powerful that it has the ability to actually limit your intimacy in other areas. Too many couples get caught in the notion that if they communicate, share, and experience a sense of union in the act of intercourse then they must have a sound relationship. This is not true. Instead, the intensity of sexual expressions pulls your attention away from the often uncomfortable and incomplete areas of your relationship that need serious work.

The act of sexual intercourse presupposes that both of you have attained the psychic and spiritual sexual identity of the marital relationship. This is the purpose of your engagement, and your wedding is the celebration of that process. A spirituality of care during your engagement proposes sexual abstinence.

If the two of you are planning to "gift" each other—for the first time—with a full expression of your sexuality on your wedding night, you will be bringing to each other a priceless gift, indeed. If, on the other hand, you already engage in sexual intercourse, consider the risks you are taking, the risk of not developing your relationship to its fullest potential prior to marriage. Ask yourselves, "Is our sexual intercourse really enhancing our relationship or are there motivations for our lovemaking that block our being even more intimate in other areas? Do we engage in intercourse because we fear we may not stay together? Do we use intercourse as a substitute for solving serious problems in our relationship? Do we use intercourse to meet some of our basic psychological needs, like being accepted and loved?"

Perhaps most of you don't need the following caution. Nonetheless, the caution is timely. Studies indicate that premarital sex is common among teenagers and young adults. If you have had sex with numerous partners, do not overrule the possibility that you are a carrier of a sexually transmitted disease. Use your engagement period to learn about each other's sexual histories; that's part of your deepening intimacy. If one of you is HIV-positive, even if contracted through a tainted blood transfusion or as a worker in a healthcare profession, and you fail to share this information, your silence is a serious violation of the trust that needs to exist in your relationship. If your honesty leads to the end of the relationship, then it's been a successful engagement; you both fully entered into the relationship to explore its lifelong potential. If you choose to continue your relationship, avail yourselves of all the educational material and medical resources that will help you both live with this dimension of your intimacy.

Affirmation: Your love for each other enables you to see the brighter side of life. When one of you tends to be cynical or sarcastic, the other will rush in to accentuate what is positive and hope-filled. Between the two of you, you grasp the whole picture rather than a narrow selected view. You don't disregard each other's weaknesses, but highlight each other's strengths. When one of you suffers a setback, the other is supporting and comforting. This is affirmation: the acceptance of another person—shortcomings, weaknesses, character flaws, and all.

Affirmation, on the surface, may sound easy. After all, you love each other; of course you affirm and accept each other. But it's not that simple; truly affirming and accepting another person requires an understanding of basic human development.

Remember what Chapters Three and Four said about understanding yourselves and each other: a great deal of history has shaped the two of you into the persons you are today, into the real you that you bring into marriage. Your home lives, your educational experiences and opportunities, your socioeconomic situations, have all fashioned your attitudes on life. When you welcome each other into your life, you welcome each other's total self and all that has formed that self. At the same time, you offer your total self and all that has formed that self. It's a mutual giving and receiving without judgment, without intentions to change each other. This is affirmation.

Your engagement signals that you are ready to be that giving and accepting. You are ready to affirm—and to be affirmed. How does this get expressed in an intimate relationship? How is affirmation manifested in engagement?

You affirm each other by not doing each other's thinking. Gene was quick-witted and outgoing. When he and Tess would go out with friends, Gene often answered questions directed at Tess. Tess felt like a child, when her parents would do the same thing. One evening, one of their friends cut Gene short: "Let Tess speak for herself." That simple comment helped Gene see exactly what he was doing and how it was affecting Tess. Although Gene wasn't able to change his behavior immediately—poor habits are hard to break—he became far more conscientious about how he and Tess interacted in a group environment. He affirmed her individuality by letting her speak for herself. Tess' self-esteem was enhanced, and their relationship reached a new level.

When you affirm each other, you eliminate stereotypical thinking. You treat each other as unique and exciting individuals. You do not make assumptions about how each other will react or what each other will say. You are on your guard against reducing each other to a label: a male chauvinist, a dizzy female, a clumsy so-and-so. As part of your engagement spirituality, you see each other as individuals and not as group members. You never cease to be surprised by each other, delighting in your own lack of assumptions.

Honesty and positive thinking are components of affirmation. For example, when you share your feelings, you are not only honest with each other but also give each other the benefit of the doubt. You do not blame each other for your feelings, you are honest about their nature and intensity. You do not falsely flatter each other, you are quick to point out each other's special talents. You never take each other for granted. Part of your engagement spirituality is to show appreciation for each other in all the small things that make up your relationship.

Affirming each other means you are sensitive to the growth that takes place in each other and in your relationship. Because your engagement period is characterized by a great deal of change—often change that is exciting and promising—you are especially sensitive to each other's accomplishments, such as new jobs, raises, and educational accomplishments. You affirm each other in the good things that happen, even when personal preferences are not met.

When Victoria got a promotion, she had to leave for two weeks of special training. This left Jeff, her fiancé, feeling both happy and sad. He was happy for Victoria, but he was sad because nothing comparable seemed to be happening to him. He was somewhat jealous of Victoria and a little threatened. As Jeff congratulated Victoria on her promotion, his heart wasn't in it.

While Victoria was away, Jeff confided his distress to a friend who suggested that Jeff imagine himself in Victoria's place. "You'd want Victoria to be happy for you, to trust you, and to believe in you."

Despite his ambivalent feelings, Jeff knew what his friend was talking about. He knew he had not affirmed Victoria, the one person he loved more than anyone. When Victoria returned, Jeff was able to listen to her account of what had gone on at the workshop. He didn't feel resentment or jealousy; he didn't feel threatened. He saw in his beloved a great potential for reaching career heights that she very much wanted. Jeff's ability to seek advice and to be aware of his feelings led him to affirm his beloved and practice the spirituality of engagement.

Love: While caring and affirming come from loving each other, love remains a unique characteristic of engagement spirituality. Expressing your affection for each other is now, and always will be, an important dimension of your relationship. Touching each other, hugging and kissing, holding hands, and sitting close are signs of your love. You enjoy being together, and that pleasure is naturally expressed in body language that says "I love us."

You also express your love with gifts: the long-standing gifts of flowers, candies, greeting cards, and symbolic trinkets that say, in a tangible way, "I love you." Flowers, for example, are nature's way of capturing what your spirit experiences. If your feelings and thoughts could take material form, they would be like flowers: delicate, colorful, fragrant. When you present each other with flowers, you are saying, "This is what my love for you looks like!" Other simple gifts like a shell from the seashore or a leaf from an autumn walk can say, "I thought of you when I noticed God's splendor surrounding me."

Love motivates you to offer these gifts. It's not something *extra* or different that you do now, during your engagement. Rather, now is the time you learn the value of such expressions and cultivate a pattern of expressing love that will wear well through the years ahead.

One night, along a desolate stretch of highway, Ken started composing a love song about his fiancée, Suzanne. It didn't make the hit parade, but it did make Ken feel, in the moment, as if Suzanne were in the car with him. When Ken got home, he wrote out the song and sent it to Suzanne—and she loved it. That simple and playful gesture allowed Suzanne to feel Ken's love across distance and time.

Reaching out: Because you love each other, your relationship as an engaged couple is a leaven in the various communities in which you interact. Your commitment to each other gives you a certain energy that can be used for the good of others. Although you had much to offer others as individuals—and still do—as a couple, your resources, especially concern and support for others, are multiplied. As a couple, you find new aspects of yourselves, new depths that were waiting to come alive with the spark of love.

The love you share during your engagement allows you to grow and stretch. Because you are more flexible during this time, you're willing to reach out beyond yourselves. You're excited about venturing into the world as a couple, ready to be all you can be for others. You are ready to hear old things in a new way; you are ready to enter life with fresh visions and great hope, for yourselves and others.

You wish others could have what you have: the love and friendship of another person you trust, a person who is there for you, a person with whom you want to share all of life. You're not embarrassed by your love, you're not burdened with the need to be secretive. You want the world to know that you love—and are loved! This energy, in turn, allows you to reach out to others who are hurting, lonely, or confused. Your love has traveled through many stages to reach this depth: commitment.

Lelia and Owen's engagement was the typical busy period of adjusting and exploring. They enjoyed nights out dancing, attending Billy Joel concerts, going to movies, and getting together with their friends. They spent countless afternoons looking for an apartment, buying furniture, and making wedding plans. But in the midst of this flurry of activity, they had time for their families, for their nieces and nephews, for their faith communities. They did volunteer work once a week in a soup kitchen and helped out with the local food pantry. Their love propelled them outward. This is engagement spirituality.

These characteristics, which are expressed in the way you act, are the substance of your engagement spirituality which becomes your sacrament of marriage. During your engagement, you have the opportunity to form patterns of caring, affirming, loving, and reaching out to others that make possible the revelation of God's goodness.

Reflecting Together

Many people are not comfortable with the word *spirituality*, but as this chapter shows, everyone has a spirituality. If someone asks you, "What are the important things you do for each other?" what would you answer?

Are there things you don't do for each other that you think you should be doing? What is your hesitation?

How is your engagement period reflecting the goodness of God to others?

Chapter 7

GETTING READY TO WELCOME CHILDREN

One of the most beautiful and most sacred aspects of your union in marriage will be your participation in the procreation of children. Your faith and trust in God and in each other will be fulfilled in flesh and blood as you, with God, bring children into the world. Your children will be your gifts to each other. Now is the time to think about what parenting means to you and what kind of parents you want to be.

When you have a baby, the direction and support of your pediatrician, parents, well-meaning friends, and the popular baby books will get you through the first months and years of parenting.

But now, during your engagement, you are building the future when "Baby makes three."

Your engagement relationship is an intense one-on-one relationship, and it's difficult to project into the future when that will no longer be the case. But the arrival of a child into your relationship will cause a great deal of change for both of you. Some couples make the transition easily; others struggle. Perhaps your attitude is "No problem. We're really looking forward to it." That's great, but let's explore some of the implications of your readiness.

Acceptance

You are ready to be parents when you accept yourselves and each other. Acceptance, however, does not suggest that there is no room for change.

As Diane got older, she realized how much like her father she was. She saw in herself many unfavorable behavior characteristics that she had noticed in her father. Diane began to isolate some of these behaviors and to concentrate on changing them. When she felt free enough to tell her boyfriend about her undesirable behaviors, she was on her way to accepting them and changing them.

Jane Anne's change came about through self-discovery. She was an assertive, not to say aggressive, young woman, who had experienced significant success in a short time in her chosen career. As Jane Anne became more successful at her work, however, she became less successful in her personal life. She wondered why she turned off Al. Gradually, it dawned on her that the assertive behavior that produced positive results at work were not appropriate in her social life. She paid attention to how the office environment was dictating her behavior after work-hours. When Jane Anne stopped treating

Al as a competitive colleague, the couple's depth of intimacy and commitment deepened.

Like Diane and Jane Anne, you may be ready for change. Take a look at the following questions. Do they suggest areas you might wish to change in yourselves, especially as you think about what kind of parents you want to be? There are no right or wrong answers. You are simply trying to discover something about yourselves that may have implications for parenting. Individually, go through the lists in this chapter, then discuss your responses together. The more you know about yourselves and each other, the more you are creating your engagement and the better prepared you will be for marriage. While you cannot foresee everything that will happen in the years ahead, you can learn to deal with what's going on in your lives now.

Do I like being alone?	❏ YES	❏ NO
Do I like being with other people?	❏ YES	❏ NO
Do people ever say I'm selfish?	❏ YES	❏ NO
Do little things upset me?	❏ YES	❏ NO
Am I often jealous?	❏ YES	❏ NO
Am I a competitive person?	❏ YES	❏ NO
Would I be a good role model as a parent?	❏ YES	❏ NO
Was adolescence a rough period for me?	❏ YES	❏ NO
Did I have a happy childhood?	❏ YES	❏ NO
Am I achievement oriented?	❏ YES	❏ NO

If one or both of you have little impulse control, if you can't roll with the ups and downs of life, if interruptions in your plans cause you great turmoil, reevaluate yourselves first as persons and then as potential parents. One mother used to go into a rage when her child spilled milk; yet, spilled milk and broken treasures go with the territory of being a parent. Parenthood will require selflessness, the ability to adapt to change, and the realization that people are more important than things. If this isn't you now, if this isn't a dimension of the way you interact as a couple, work on it. Your children will someday appreciate it.

The Process of Change

Success in your relationship depends on your individual emotional health. If you like yourselves as individuals, if you accept yourselves, if you function free from major periods of anxiety, frustration, and depression, the odds for a successful union are high. If, on the other hand, your levels of maturity are questionable, if you are too detached from the needs of others, if your needs are paramount and exclusive, if you are self-centered and selfish, the success of your union is at risk.

If you want to change your behavior, start with where you are emotionally right now. Change happens only when you know where or what you are now and where you want to go or what you want to be later.

What you do to generate change, however, is up to you. Talking to a significant person in your life is often helpful; that person's honest insights and suggestions can give you a clear view of what you need to change and how. On the other hand, you may consider input from a person trained in the helping professions: a counselor, psychologist, or psychiatrist. A spiritual director is another source of honesty and discipline that can help you change.

There is tremendous opportunity for growth and change in the daily interactions between the two of you. In choosing each other, you have affirmed each other's unique personhood. Because you feel yourselves cherished, you are able to trust your relationship to point out weaknesses to you, as individuals and as a couple. Consider the following scenario.

Geraldine liked Hal's easy-going manner, but she got frightened when he got behind the wheel of a car. With very little provocation, Hal would become angry with other drivers, sometimes to the point of trying to "get revenge." Geraldine begged Hal to be more patient, to be more tolerant, but he vehemently defended his actions. Even when Geraldine tried to appeal to Hal's sense of care for her, Hal persisted in his aggressive driving.

Before he becomes a parent, Hal is going to have to deal with this angry side of his personality that comes to the surface when he gets behind the wheel of a car. To change, Hal needs more than will power; he needs to accept the fact that he harbors some kind of anger. He may want to explore the reasons for this anger to see if there are connections to past experiences or if the anger is part of his basic life orientation. Hal probably does not need professional help; he simply needs to ask himself some hard questions about his anger as a driver.

Geraldine is right to protest Hal's driving habits; her life is at risk, Hal's life is at risk, the lives of other drivers and pedestrians are at risk—the life of an infant in the car with Hal will be at risk. When he's behind the wheel, Hal is not creating a safe environment for anyone, let alone an infant.

Geraldine can help Hal change. *Before getting into the car with Hal*, Geraldine can ask Hal to remain calm and patient. *Before getting into the car with Hal*, Geraldine can draw Hal's attention to some of the near mishaps they've had in the past when his anger as a driver caused him to use poor judgment. *Before getting into the car with Hal*, Geraldine has a greater chance of getting through to Hal. He is more likely to hear her concern and fear *before he gets into the car*.

Geraldine and Hal are preparing to be responsible parents. They are eliminating a behavior that could endanger their future children, but there's more; they are learning the role that self-acceptance plays in a specific situation. Geraldine loves Hal; she accepts him and cherishes his life. She invites him to change a behavior that needs to be changed. Hal, accepting himself and respecting the love that Geraldine has for him, will take responsibility for his impulsive behavior and work at changing it. His wanting to stay in his relationship with Geraldine will motivate him to work on his negative behavior.

Perhaps there are parts of you that you cannot change, parts that you have to learn to accept and live with in ways that are not destructive. The story of Rambhu and the tiger illustrates how this is possible.

The villagers captured a tiger and brought it to Rambhu. As the village keeper, Rambhu caged the animal. Although Rambhu was friendly and gentle with the tiger, the tiger roared whenever Rambhu came near—even with food.

Rambhu was afraid of the tiger. He admitted his fear to himself and to God. In prayer, he asked God to tame the tiger. There was little change in the tiger's behavior, however, and one day a village girl got too close to the tiger's cage. She was badly hurt.

Rambhu put the tiger into a pit and put a fence around the pit to keep the tiger away from the villagers and to keep the villagers away from the tiger. The tiger roared day and night, giving Rambhu very little rest and peace. Once again, Rambhu prayed to God: "Please take this tiger from us. Let it die before it does more harm."

To Rambhu's surprise, God answered, "Rambhu, bring the tiger into your house, and let it choose its own room." Faithfully,

Rambhu went to the pit and threw a ladder down. Up scrambled the tiger. The two stared at each other as if their eyes were locked in a duel. Rambhu had no fear because God had ordered him to do this. The tiger finally lay down at Rambhu's feet.

For some time, the tiger stayed outside Rambhu's house, roaring every night, all night, and frightening Rambhu. Finally, he let the tiger come into his house. Rambhu had no fear because God had ordered him to do this. Again, Rambhu locked eyes with the tiger to show that he was not afraid of who the tiger was. This routine went on day after day, night after night.

After a few years, the tiger and Rambhu became good friends. Rambhu would touch the tiger and playfully put his hand in its mouth. All the villagers were amazed. They sensed that Rambhu and the tiger were in some way bonded together and that each had learned how to get along with the other. But they also noticed that Rambhu never dared to take his eyes off the tiger.

Like Rambhu and the tiger, learn to get along with those parts of yourselves that you can't change—and change those parts that you can. As you undergo the process of change, be gentle with yourselves. Change what you can, but be tolerant of your limitations. Granted, will power is part of the process but so is acceptance, as Rambhu and the tiger indicate. Accepting those parts of yourselves that you don't seem able to change is a way of overcoming their hold over you. That is self-acceptance and other-acceptance.

The Act of Accepting

You are ready to be parents if you are accepting of other persons. Your decision to become engaged was a great moment of acceptance. That's why this time is so exhilarating and exciting; you feel loved and treasured by the one you love and treasure.

Now, as a couple, the two of you form a social unit, a unit that is preparing you to become a family. Once you are part of a social unit, conflicts arise when your personal needs collide. This will become acute when children enter your social unit.

The needs of infants and children are so compelling that adult needs have to be put on hold. Now, during your engagement, assess your desire and ability to balance your needs as a couple and as a social unit in relationship to others. Individually, review the following questions, and then discuss your answers together.

Do my partner and I communicate well?	❏ YES	❏ NO
Do I decide how we spend weekends?	❏ YES	❏ NO
Am I patient when others need my time?	❏ YES	❏ NO
Am I caring when someone is sick?	❏ YES	❏ NO
Do I think of children as a burden?	❏ YES	❏ NO
Did I fight a lot with my siblings?	❏ YES	❏ NO
Will my partner make a good parent?	❏ YES	❏ NO
Do I enjoy baby-sitting?	❏ YES	❏ NO
Do I enjoy the company of my parents?	❏ YES	❏ NO
Will I be happy if we have no children?	❏ YES	❏ NO

Remember, there are no right or wrong answers. Some answers, however, might be more revelatory than others with regard to how ready you are to be parents. As you read the following scenario, notice the different personality traits in Cosmo and Theodora that will cause them problems when they become parents.

Before their engagement, Cosmo and Theodora had never really seen how each other lived. Cosmo was always meticulously groomed and thought that all women were, by nature, neat and tidy. He could not tolerate personal uncleanliness. Whenever he and Theodora went out, Theodora was always radiantly beautiful. Cosmo had no way of knowing that when she emerged from her bedroom at her parent's home, Theodora left behind a mess or strewn clothing, cosmetics, jewelry, and hair-care products.

Fortunately, during their engagement, Cosmo began to suspect that his fiancée's regard for order and cleanliness did not match his. When Theodora ate, she managed to spill something on the table or on herself. In the car, she shredded paper wrappings from candy and casually discarded them on the floor. Cosmo especially disliked Theodora's habit of chewing on a toothpick at the end of a meal and discarding it…wherever. It dawned on Cosmo that he and Theodora were going to form an odd couple, like Oscar Madison and Felix Unger. He wasn't at all happy about that.

Finally, Cosmo confronted Theodora with her sloppiness. They argued, and later Cosmo felt bad and regretted that he had hurt his beloved. Yet, he knew how important order and tidiness were to him. Theodora went home and complained to her brothers and sister about Cosmo's behavior: "He called me everything but a slob."

Cosmo called Theodora later that night. For hours, they talked about the confrontation they'd had, their feelings, their individual habits of cleanliness, and their desire to find a way to work through the conflict. Their conversation gradually led to humor as they both saw their own extremes. Cosmo began to see that his standards were perhaps too rigid and that his image of all women being models of neatness was an illusion. He loved Theodora. He could accept that he projected something important to him onto her. Theodora began to see that "carefree" didn't have to mean "careless," but she admitted that change would be difficult for her—if not impossible. She loved Cosmo, though, and asked him to be patient with her as she tried to become more conscientious.

This relationship survived conflicting values because Cosmo and Theodora successfully negotiated their differences. Cosmo became more accepting of Theodora, whose large bustling family did not foster all the niceties of etiquette. Theodora learned how much neatness meant to Cosmo and resolved to do better.

Cosmo and Theodora showed flexibility. Because they accepted the core goodness of each other, and because they knew their own needs and limitations, they were able to enter a conflict situation and find their relationship stronger than ever.

Your ability to accept each other's differences is tested in your relationship. Having a mutually accepting attitude boosts your respective self-esteem and creates a pleasant and loving atmosphere. As you become more accepting, you move away from rigid patterns of behavior and unrealistic assumptions.

This accepting stance prepares you for parenthood, for nothing *demands* flexibility like a baby. The child's health, temperament, and schedule will challenge the two of you not only to accept the child but to accept each other's attempts to parent. A baby will need you to be flexible and accepting of his or her behavior as you create a healthy and loving home environment, which to some extent is an objective extension of the relationship you are creating with each other—especially during your engagement.

Of course, Cosmo and Theodora are probably going to have a problem. Theodora may well have the philosophy that a clean child is not a happy child. From her point of view, a child is only happy when rolling around on the ground or making mud pies. Cosmo, who has a tendency to see germs everywhere, has a different view on cleanliness. This difference, which they are aware of as an engaged couple, is going to get magnified when they have children. If Theodora is wise, she'll take Cosmo on a walk through a park where he can see how children of all ages enjoy themselves in the sand and dust of an active playground.

Interacting With Children

During your engagement, you have countless opportunities to see yourselves, as individuals and as a couple, around children. Granted, many people have little tolerance for other people's children, but when they have their own, their tolerance level skyrockets.

Frank thought of babies and small children as "willful adults who wanted their own way." He took mean delight in frustrating small children, feeling satisfied when they "learned their lesson, that they won't always get what they want." Frank had no appreciation for what childhood is all about—and even less of an understanding for what parenthood is all about. He shuddered each time his married sister asked him to "hold the baby."

Does Frank sound like either of you, to some degree? During your engagement, you can begin to appreciate children by noticing how they explore their environment, how they move rapidly from stage to stage in their development, and how long a period of nurture they need before they grow up. Spend time with your nieces, nephews, godchildren, and your friends' children. Try to be sensitive to their needs as children. Let patience and tolerance be hallmarks of the rapport you build with these children. Note, too, that there is a correlation between the way you treat each other and the way you treat children.

The Role of Generosity

You are ready to be parents when you understand what it means to be generous. This is not a generosity associated with giving lavish gifts. Rather, relationship generosity refers to a goodness of spirit. What are you ready to do for each other for the good of your relationship? What are you willing to do purely for the good of each other? How forgiving are you? How much effort do you put into pleasing each other? How far are you willing to go to preserve your relationship? Individually, review the following questions, and then discuss your answers together.

Do I sulk when I am forced to change my plans?	❏ YES	❏ NO
Do I think that a mother's place is in the home?	❏ YES	❏ NO
Do I think that boys are more difficult to manage than girls?	❏ YES	❏ NO
Would I rather parent girls than boys?	❏ YES	❏ NO
Am I willing to change diapers?	❏ YES	❏ NO
Do I think that children cry only to get attention?	❏ YES	❏ NO
Do I enjoy socializing with my friends?	❏ YES	❏ NO
Do I spend money on necessities only?	❏ YES	❏ NO
Do I believe that sparing the rod will spoil the child?	❏ YES	❏ NO

The answers to these questions highlight your generosity. For example, let's look briefly at the last statement in the list. Spanking and slapping are not "generous" forms of discipline. When parents resort to physical forms of discipline, they are, in fact, not disciplining; they are punishing. They are reacting, almost out of habit, to the forms of "discipline" they were exposed to as children themselves. They have not taken the time to explore their own feelings of fear or frustration, and instead, have responded in reflex fashion. They have not remained generous with their child.

Forming a "Welcoming" Mentality

What can you do to form a "welcoming" mentality? Be willing to give without counting the cost. Parenting is not a part-time responsibility, and children are not always agreeable and pleasant. They express the same types of moods, emotional peaks and valleys, frustrations, and poor behavior that adults express. As parents, you will have to adapt to the needs of your children—for many years. This does not mean that your needs are not important. Rather, it means that in practice, some of your needs will become secondary for extended periods of time.

Share your childhood stories. Tell each other about how you interacted with your parents. Talk about what was positive and negative in those interactions. Identify the things you thought your parents did right, and permit yourselves the freedom to comment on what you think they didn't do so well. Remember, this conversation stays within the intimate safety of your relationship; you don't share parts of this conversation with future in-laws, for example. Nor do you use this conversation to "parent-bash." Rather, you share your childhoods as a means of preparing yourselves and your relationship to welcome a child.

Once you've shared your childhoods, discuss the number of children you'd like to welcome into your relationship. Do you care if you have boys or girls? What are your hopes and dreams for your children? Even if there is a certain air of unreality in this conversation, you are taking a look at a part of your future that is going to be most challenging and rewarding.

During their engagement, Mabel and Sydney talked a great deal about the family they wanted to have. They talked about how many children they wanted, what kind of community and neighborhood they'd like to raise their family in, what kind of education they wanted for their children, and even how they viewed grandparenting. When they got married, however, Mabel and Sydney were unable to have children. Although this was a disappointment for them, they were ready to deal with it; they had talked about children and family throughout their engagement. Eventually, Mabel and Sydney decided to adopt. In this way, they realized some of their engagement hopes and dreams. They had entered marriage with the mutual desire to "have" children; they were willing to welcome these children in whatever way God provided.

Part of your discussion and preparation to welcome children into your life must include finances. Consider the costs of having, raising, and educating a child. What does your medical insurance package look like? You may want to change jobs if you have inadequate coverage. If you are not accustomed to managing money, start now. Your local library has books on every aspect of parenting. The reality is, it *costs* to bring children into the world and be responsible for them into their adult years. Their health needs, education needs, and daily needs are all heavy drains on your financial resources.

Good parenting doesn't just happen. It is a learned behavior that requires thought and planning. Good parenting takes into account your child's needs, as well as your personal, individual needs and the needs of your relationship. Good parenting requires a certain amount of skill, and the bookstores are full of guides. Good parenting requires a loving marriage.

Transmitting Values to Your Children

When you're in love, it's difficult to think beyond your relationship. After all, you're both excited about the life you're now sharing and the one you are building for the future. You delight in each other and spend countless hours planning for the big day and the years to follow.

Children, however, are part of your future. The more culturally and religiously similar the two of you are, the more you may assume about parenting, especially after you've shared your individual childhood memories.

Assuming that your acceptance of children is complete, explore the child-rearing practices you will exercise as you transmit a value system to your children. To learn a solid value system, children need a secure and consistent environment, meaning the two of you do not confuse your children with mixed messages. As parents, you will speak to your children with one voice on serious matters. This does not mean that you agree on every issue. Rather, you agree on priorities, goals, and aspirations.

If you come from different cultural and/or religious traditions, you may tend to avoid discussing how these differences will affect your relationship over the years, especially when children become part of your life. You may not want to anticipate conflicts about which religion your children will be raised in, which holidays you will celebrate as a family, and which cultural traditions you will foster. A tendency to avoid such discussions, however, is only putting inevitable conflicts on hold, conflicts that can become highly volatile in a matter of a few years.

Josh was a nonpracticing Jew who had renounced his pious parents' religious practices. He had no objection to Helen having their child baptized. How was he to know that ten years into the marriage he was going to yearn to renew his own faith journey and to share that with his children? Josh's conversion back to the Judaism of his youth rocked his marriage.

Is there any way that Josh and Helen could have anticipated this eventuality while they were engaged? Maybe not. They had assumed there was going to be no problem since Josh had lost interest in the faith of his childhood. Yet, as we pointed out in an earlier chapter, your upbringing affects you throughout your entire lives. Josh and Helen could have had a conversation about "what if." They could have avoided labels about their religious orientations, such as "I'm Christian and he's Jewish." They could have examined the dimensions of their relationship that seemed to conflict with their upbringing. For example, was Josh drawn to Helen because she symbolized a sense of independence for him, a way of breaking away from what he was, at the time, no longer interested in being part of?

Together and as individuals, you have bedrock convictions about many things. These represent your values. Some of these values you absorbed from your parents. Others you assimilated from your educational experiences, your faith traditions, the mass media, and many other avenues. Unfortunately, your values will not always bear the same weight over the years. What is important to one of you now may not be so important in three years. Because of these important variables, acceptance and flexibility in your relationship are crucial.

The following questions focus on values. Individually, review them, and then discuss your answers together.

Is money really important to our relationship?	❏ YES	❏ NO
Is it okay to lie a little on a résumé to get a job?	❏ YES	❏ NO
Do women raise the children and men discipline them?	❏ YES	❏ NO
Will good sex settle all disputes we will have?	❏ YES	❏ NO
If my spouse makes me jealous, can I make him or her jealous?	❏ YES	❏ NO
Are do-gooders fools?	❏ YES	❏ NO
Do people cause their own poverty?	❏ YES	❏ NO
Do I want the children I have to be like me?	❏ YES	❏ NO
Is the man the head of the family and the woman the heart?	❏ YES	❏ NO
When we marry, do I want to live close to my parents?	❏ YES	❏ NO

These questions are designed to help you think through what is important to you. After you've shared your responses, ask yourselves, "Has our individual religious training influenced the way we responded to any of these statements? Do we claim to have a worldly wisdom that clashes with the teachings of Jesus about loving our neighbor or seeking first the kingdom of God? Are the values we see revealed to us here values that we will want to pass on to our children?"

In the final analysis, there is only so much the two of you can do during your engagement to prepare to welcome children. But you can prepare the environment of your relationship and the environment of your living conditions. With regard to the psychological and practical repercussions of a child entering your life, there is little you can plan on with certainty—other than change.

Reflecting Together

The exercises in this chapter have led you to consider many dimensions of your relationship as you anticipate welcoming children. Review these questions. Do they lead you to formulate your own questions?

What joys do each of you look forward to as a parent? Are your anticipations the same or different? Why?

What sacrifices will each of you have to make as you attempt to parent with love? Are your anticipations the same or different? Why?

BUILDING RELATIONSHIP SKILLS

n ewspaper editors tell us that the most popular columns in the religious and secular press give advice to people in love. You're probably familiar with many of them. Perhaps you've even written to these columnists for advice.

Often these columns make sweeping generalizations about marriage, offering a number of platitudes that completely miss the central point at issue. Since the columnist does not know the particular background of the person seeking help, there is a real danger that the mass-packaged advice might actually prove more harmful than helpful. Marriage counselors often meet people who have tried desperately to save their marriages by applying some formula they've read in a column, only to find that the advice complicated the situation further. Every relationship reflects the union of two very different persons with diverse backgrounds and all kinds of emotional baggage, thereby making the simple application of a set formula impossible.

These columns, together with TV talk shows that highlight marital breakups, add to the anxiety that many persons may have as they contemplate marriage. Statistics indicate that fifty percent of first marriages in the United States still fail. This is an alarming figure since it represents only those couples who "officially" dissolve their marriage; it says nothing of the countless marriages that hang together by a fragile thread. It says nothing about those marriages that are life-draining rather than life-giving. After all, an "intact" marriage does not mean it's a good marriage. In fact, the very reasons why couples in failed marriages stay together may well be a serious emotional problem. Some couples stay together to avoid hurting their parents or children, to avoid financial risks, to avoid social stigmas. These situations are usually a living hell for all involved. There is no respect, intimacy, trust, laughter, or life.

Certainly, the goal of all counselors, consciously or unconsciously, is to attempt to find a variety of ways to keep a marriage together. Sometimes this is impossible. But it is possible to point out some of the pitfalls of relationships which, if avoided, can help make your relationship not only lasting but also more fulfilling.

Psychological Attitudes and Skills

The following recommendations are based on sound psychological theories for mental wellness and healthy interpersonal relating. Consider how you can concentrate on these recommendations during your engagement.

Have an open regard for change. Never take your relationship for granted. Be ready to deal with the subtle—and often not so subtle—changes that impact the way you relate. Changes in circumstance, such as a new job, moving to a new area, or the death of a loved one, can affect the way you are currently interacting.

Ask yourselves, "What changes are going on around us right now? How do we feel, individually, about these changes? How do we see these changes impacting the way we relate? How might similar changes impact us as a married couple? as parents?" If you take stock of your relationship on a regular basis during your engagement, you will not be taken by surprise when you face a similar change later. If you see a movement in an unfavorable direction, do something about it now. Otherwise, backed into a corner, your reactions become less than you would like them to be.

No matter how busy you are right now, no matter how good things appear to be at the moment, find the time for taking stock of your relationship. This doesn't have to be a heavy conversation. One couple went out for a "just-the-two-of-us" date every Friday night. They found a quiet place to enjoy dinner and talk over the week's events. They looked at how these events influenced their relationship.

If you look at the way your relationship progressed from the moment you first met until now, you'll see that your relationship has not been static. In fact, if it were static, you probably wouldn't be engaged. Notice how the changes in your lives and in your relationship have been surrounded by points of stability. You have been changing, perhaps without knowing it.

When Jack lost his job, he felt devastated. He and Patricia were going to be married in four months. When Patricia reassured Jack that they were going to make it, Jack didn't feel so bad. Patricia's attitude taught him something about how to situate this unexpected change in their lives. He learned how important it is to consider his beloved's emotions first, and then the practical details later.

As an exercise, look through your respective family photo albums. Notice the pictures of yourselves, spaced every couple of years as you grew up. Then get pictures that show you together over the period of your relationship. Spend a night alone, or with friends or family, looking at these pictures. The physical changes you've both gone through are obvious. Looking at the physical changes will cause you to naturally consider the emotional changes that time and change have brought.

Remember how your interests and tastes changed as you got older, matured, moved to a new location, or found new friends. Certain core things were essential to you, but other things changed as your circumstances changed. If a change was quick, perhaps it was unsettling and you needed time to adjust. What kind of a change was that and would you, as individuals, find the same kind of change unsettling today? How would that same kind of change affect your relationship? If the change was a serious one, like the death of a family member or close friend or an illness, did you rely on the support of your loved ones to help get you through your grief? What or who would you and your relationship rely on today if the same change occurred?

As you enjoy your photo albums, ask yourselves what has carried over into the present. Share the stories that are behind your favorite pictures; why are certain pictures especially important to you? Do they capture something that is still important to you today?

This exercise gives you an insight into how you have changed and how you react to change. You will see an underlying continuity. Think of change not as negative but as something positive offering a new opportunity. If you're not happy with the way you've dealt with change in the past, learn from your unhappiness. How would the two of you handle that same change today, as a couple?

At Carol and David's rehearsal party, everyone enjoyed a videotape that Carol's sister had put together. She had taken their photographs from birth to romance and put them on videotape with appropriate headings. It was a special moment for everyone because it captured the life journey of two people, separately and then together, on the eve of their wedding. Change never looked more real and more hopeful.

Express your feelings honestly. This point has been emphasized repeatedly in previous chapters. Talk about what is important to you as individuals and what is important to you as a couple. During your engagement, let your feelings be known. Open and honest expression of feelings helps each of you know exactly what's going on in the emotional system of your relationship. Open communication prevents you from expecting each other to be a mind reader. The old you-would-know-if-you-really-loved-me attitude is a dangerous myth. Even after years of marriage, you will never automatically know each other's feelings.

Women are much more apt than men to express their feelings. To their disadvantage, many men find it difficult to express feelings or express them in inappropriate ways. Jack is an example. He is an even-tempered person who puts up with things he really doesn't like. With no forewarning, however, he will blow up and say, "I've had it! I can't stand this any longer!" Any woman in a relationship with Jack will be taken completely by surprise with Jack's outbursts; he doesn't share his emotions.

Ask your parents and friends how they handle their emotions. How do others in relationship express their feelings and deal with differences? How are the women's responses different from the men's? How do your own responses align with the way others react?

Learning how to express your feelings appropriately will have a freeing effect on your relationship. Remember, you need never apologize for feelings; feelings just are. "You shouldn't feel that way" is not an appropriate, respectful, or loving response to feelings shared. Such a response negates the tremendous worth of a feeling. It inhibits the next expression of feelings.

How honestly you express your feelings to each other is an indication of the value you place on your relationship. Sharing your feelings with mutual interest and respect is your way of saying to each other, "You are my beloved and all of you, including your emotions, is important to me." This isn't the total picture, of course, but this is an important step along the way to a strong relationship. Now, during your engagement, take stock at how well you are communicating.

The feeling of mutual satisfaction reflects the level of bonding you have achieved in your interpersonal relationship. If the bonding between you is seriously flawed, a sound and long-lasting marriage is questionable. If you cannot achieve a satisfactory bond with each other now, reconsider your intention to marry—and consider your engagement a success.

Accept each other's limitations. Being realistic about each other's limitations is critical to your relationship. In addition to expressing your feelings appropriately, accept the limitations imposed by your personalities. Neither of you can be what you do not have the personality to become. For example, Ed noticed how Donna enjoyed Harry's antics at parties. But when Ed played the clown, Donna felt embarrassed. She explained to Ed that Harry seemed to have a gift for making people laugh. "I like that in Harry," she explained, "but I'm going to marry you because you have the gift of being sensitive and serious about important things. I don't expect you to be the life of the party." Ed felt grateful to Donna because she lifted a burden from his shoulders. She let him know that their relationship wasn't threatened simply because he had different gifts.

It can happen that a particular personality trait has nothing to do with personal limits but more to do with the way a person developed socially. Fred could have been a character in a wisecracking sitcom. He made light of every situation. This was part of his charm and what he thought people expected of him. But, while Betty laughed with him, she didn't like it. This aspect of Fred's charm had a way of wearing thin. Betty actually found it monotonous. This is where honesty with herself came into play. Denying that Fred's shortcoming bothered her would be, at best, a temporary solution. Fortunately, Betty sensed that someday she would have to admit the truth. She knew that by coming to grips with this personality trait, her relationship with Fred would become stronger and more honest over the years.

But Betty had to be careful; offering criticism, even loving criticism, is a delicate endeavor. Betty suspected that Fred's wisecracking was a technique he used to protect himself from getting emotionally involved. She didn't tell him this, but at important times, she used his wisecrack as an opportunity to ask what he really thought about a situation. She found that he really cared deeply about the things he was joking about. If she had taken a different approach, like "Honey, do you mind if I tell you something I don't like about you," Fred may have counterattacked. It could have led to a major argument.

If particular shortcomings bother you so much that your relationship is disturbed, look closely at the tension. In most cases, behavior becomes more pronounced with advancing years; it won't become easier to cope with later on. Recognize the limits in your individual personalities and in each other's. Realize that dealing with these limits takes patience and understanding. Don't be surprised if you discover that some of the very things you complain about in each other are traits you both possess. Once you get in touch with this, compassion and patience are soon to follow.

As you consider your limits, look honestly at your social life, professional life, personal life, family life. Do either of you tend to embrace a "superachiever" mentality, expecting tremendous feats of yourself or each other or your relationship? Such a mentality ultimately brings a heavy burden to the life you are building.

A good rule of thumb is "balance in all things." When your respective roles and responsibilities as social, professional, and family people are balanced with your personal limits, your relationship will evolve into a naturally balanced dynamic. When you respect each other's limits, the foundation for a long and satisfying marriage is put in place.

Share your dreams. A good relationship that reflects optimism, trust, and openness allows for change while you both grow into more mature, self-confident people. It also allows each of you to be expansive in terms of dreams and aspirations. Your dreams allow you to imagine your future before you get there. If you have no dreams, what are you aiming for? Use your dreams for discovering what is important to you and how you can make it happen.

Express your dreams in such a way that respects your mutual goal: a shared life. Do not impose your individual dreams on each other.

For some of you, this may be a new way of thinking about your life as a couple. Consider this: for most of your life, you have been preparing for your own individual careers. As individuals, you've had hopes and aspirations. Now, you come together. You are no longer two individual sets of hopes and aspirations; you are a couple planning a shared life. Your engagement period gives you the opportunity to bring these hopes and aspirations together, to pull from your respective experiences, and dream anew.

Now is the time to establish goals as a couple. What difference is your marriage going to make to the world? It is normal to think that your goals are covered by your wanting to be the best family you can be and raising your children well. This is good, but it focuses on your internal environment only. What will be your external effect on society?

Before they got married, Henrietta and Dave decided that they wanted to start their life together by giving something to society. They volunteered to spend two years as guest workers in Kenya, Africa, helping to educate elementary school children. There they had their first child. When they returned to the United States, they took an active role in local politics. They had established such a strong relationship during their engagement that they were able to carry out this challenging start to their marriage.

As an engaged couple, Randy and Martha became active in their parish community as catechists. After they were married, they saw a need for adult education in the area of marriage. They organized a program that brought in guest speakers and used their home as a welcoming place for the speakers.

It is natural for you to think only about what your life together within your home will be like. Yet, your engagement is a time of dreaming, when you look beyond yourselves to what your relationship offers society.

When you first start thinking about this, be expansive. Don't cut short your dreaming by interjecting objections and limitations. Allow your imaginations to take in a broad array of possibilities. Then, and only then, evaluate your dreams and see how you can make some of them realities.

Keep your love alive. A good relationship is characterized by love. This is not some unrealistic romantic notion of love, but a respect for each other and a desire to achieve some degree of contentment and peace in the emotional warmth and affection you share.

Love is unselfish; it is open and able to meet the needs of others. But, the nature of love may change, even die. A loss of love is something most people would rather deny, but the reality of it is ever present. Love gone astray may turn into hatred, or worse, indifference. We are especially capable of hurting those persons to whom we can also bring great happiness.

Songwriters capitalize on the themes of lost and unrequited love. One reason for this is that everyone has experienced some degree of rejection in life; it's easy to identify with tales of rejection. The rejection may be real or imagined and may result from a one-sided love affair, but all people seem capable of relating to it.

This alerts you to the importance of reciprocal love in your relationship. Take time to do things for each other. A good example of how love can be nurtured in an active way as a joint effort is the engagement shower. Aileen knew how to make occasions memorable. When she was asked to host Georgia's shower, nothing was left to chance. Georgia's boyfriend, Bob, volunteered to do whatever he could to help. The shower was a win-win situation for everybody. Georgia's happiness with the shower made Bob happy. He felt good about his own participation. He had given of himself, in a special way, for enjoyment of his beloved.

Lovers are "for" each other on a daily basis. They do things for each other with attention and affection. They express their gratitude for the goodness they find in each other; their relationship brings them mutual joy. They are conscientious about promoting each other's well-being and happiness.

Sherry and Norman found a unique way to do this during engagement. When they were separated by Norman's service in the army, they put their thoughts in a notebook—one notebook—instead of exchanging love letters. Sherry wrote and drew things in the notebook and mailed it to Norman. Norman enjoyed Sherry's presence on the pages of the notebook, formed responses—in the notebook—added things that Sherry could respond to, and mailed the notebook back to her. This continued until they filled the notebook. They expressed their deepest thoughts, their emotions, and their experiences of the day. Their notebook contained poems, dreams, anxieties, and all the other things lovers share. The notebook served the purpose of their being present to each other even when they were separated.

Like Norman and Sherry, you probably have your own special ways of deepening your love relationship as you move toward your marriage vows. Don't let these special expressions fade away after marriage. The purpose they serve today remains just as important in the years to come, for you will always be lovers.

Spiritual Attitudes and Skills

When you get married in the Catholic Church, the pastor of your parish has the responsibility of seeing that you are prepared for a Christian marriage. He will inquire into your religious views and practices.

Some engaged couples are uncomfortable with the pastor's questions because it makes them feel that someone outside their love relationship is checking up on them in an area they consider their own business. Actually, this inquiry is something much more profound than a casual checking up. Your pastor's responsibility is to help you take into account all that will affect your marriage. In particular, because you have chosen to celebrate your marriage in a religious ceremony, the pastor wants you to realize the significant positive impact that the rites of the Church can have on your life.

Previous chapters have emphasized the spiritual meanings and transformational possibilities that religious faith brings to your relationship. The sacramental life of the Church offers you many unique opportunities for enhancing your spiritual attitudes and skills.

Develop a eucharistic spirituality. When two Catholics marry, they usually celebrate their marriage at the Eucharist. Among other names, the Church's eucharistic meal has been called a banquet of *love*, the celebration of the *covenant* of Jesus Christ, the eucharistic *sacrifice*, and holy *Communion*. These names for Eucharist show its importance both for Christian engagement and Christian marriage.

Each day is an opportunity for you to live the covenant of your mutual love. The intense experience of being for each other often entails sacrifice that leads to greater spiritual union. Eucharistic themes and relationship themes go together. You can bring your relationship to the celebration of the Eucharist. Here's how.

The opening penitential rite gives you an opportunity to reflect briefly on how you have treated each other and your families and friends during the week. If there have been any failings, you have the opportunity to acknowledge them, determine to do better, and know that this conversion of heart is exactly what God wishes.

The appointed scriptural readings will invariably address some aspect of your life that needs attention. A popular saying has it that Scripture comforts the afflicted and afflicts the comfortable. The Word of God, never outdated, has reference to our lives, either as individuals or as part of a community. As an engaged couple, listen to what Scripture says to your relationship. Listen to the invitation to love that it offers.

For example, consider Jesus' parables of a treasure hidden in a field or of the mustard seed. Hear these parables through the experience of your relationship. The themes of growth, delight, and of giving up everything for a purpose are well suited to the bond you share. Talk about the scriptural readings and the priest's homily to see how the gospel applies to your life.

When you pray the Our Father, hear yourselves say, "Forgive us our trespasses as we forgive those who trespass against us." At the sign of peace, extend the joy and peace of your relationship to those around you. The customary handshake or embrace is an important external gesture as you prepare to receive the Eucharist, referred to as the Lamb of God, who takes away the sins of the world. The reception of the Eucharist is communion with Jesus, who died for our sins.

In all these ways, the Eucharist allows you to bring a sense of purpose and reconciliation to your lives. These are all opportunities for you to bring the gospel into your life precisely as an engaged couple. More than ever before, you may discover how meaningful all of these are and how some of them may have been previously carried out in a mechanical way.

If you are in an interreligious relationship and only one of you can receive the Eucharist because of the present regulations of the Church, the other can reflect on all these meanings during the time of Communion. If not being able to participate in Communion is a hardship for you, it does reflect accurately that your religious convictions are not the same. But there is an important positive aspect to this situation. Your presence together is a real support and points to your desire to overcome all obstacles to your being united.

Become active reconcilers. Every engaged couple must learn to heal the wounds caused by serious disagreements and fights. Throughout life, you will experience periods of great togetherness and great disagreement. Arriving late for a party, one wife said, only half-jokingly it seemed, "We almost ended twenty years of marriage over whether we should have taken a right- or left-hand turn."

It is important to be aware of the steps needed to restore a relationship that has been seriously threatened by intemperate words or deeds. Sometimes after a healing has taken place, one person will say, "I felt like killing you." The words are not an exaggeration. When confronted with someone who seems to be totally opposed to us and wounds us to the core, we are often far from kind with our feelings toward that person. Fortunately, few of us act on these feelings. But we recognize the feelings and try to lighten them with casual comments.

A film called *The War of the Roses* actually had its two stars, Kathleen Turner and Michael Douglas, end their family feud in self-annihilation with their fall from a chandelier, their final battleground. Is this what happens to people who know nothing about conflict resolution? No, but as a modern parable, it does illustrate what can happen when we do not know how to read properly the signs of disintegration in a relationship.

How well are you using your engagement period to foster your relationship and heal whatever hurts you may cause each other? Time is not some vast reservoir from which you can draw when you need to. It is limited and runs out for each and every one of us. Attentiveness to the importance of using time wisely in creating your relationship is a mark of maturity. Overseeing the relationship, taking time to repair it when it has been wounded, and seeking an ever deeper union are all worth your time.

This work of reconciliation is brought into the life of the Church through the sacrament of reconciliation. The sacrament of reconciliation builds on the reconciliation that you achieve in your relationship on a day-to-day basis. When you experience reconciliation, your relationship is strengthened while you participate in fulfilling the gospel message that Jesus preached.

The sacrament of reconciliation can thus play an important role in your preparation for marriage. The message of Jesus is that our sins need not doom us to despair, that there is a way out of the cycle of destruction. Sins are to be repented and forgiven, and the sinner is to be lifted up. This is why everyone loves the story of the Prodigal Son.

As part of his pastoral care for you, your pastor may invite you to participate in the sacrament of reconciliation. This is a unique opportunity for you to consider your individual lives and your plans for a life together. You can review your personal strengths and see where you need help. You can praise God for the compassion you experience through the ministry of the Church and for the healing forgiveness you receive in the sacrament of reconciliation. After participating in the sacrament, you may, as many people do, experience a newness about your relationship, as love fills your spirit.

The sacrament of reconciliation is particularly appropriate if you have felt alienated for one reason or another from the Church. Naomi had a lot of anger with the Church. Naomi wanted nothing to do with a church wedding, but her parents and Marty's parents put pressure on her. At their first meeting, Father Louis picked up on Naomi's hurt and anger. Over the course of several sessions, he went over the events that had caused Naomi's disillusion, was able to empathize with her, and to talk to her about the need for the healing of these memories. After going through several stages of remembering and healing with Naomi, Father Louis suggested that a good way to mark newfound peace was to celebrate it in the sacrament of reconciliation. Naomi agreed, and Father Louis placed his hands on her head and said the prayer of absolution. Naomi felt grateful to Father Louis, who strove to make the encounter between himself and Naomi an authentic human one that allowed her to experience the compassion of the merciful God through the ministry of the Church.

During the year, there are also communal celebrations of reconciliation with individual confession. Oftentimes, these are at the end of Lent or Advent. They are considered a serious time of sacramental reconciliation in the Church's preparation for the coming feast of Easter or Christmas. Engaged couples who assist at these services are showing the importance of reconciliation in their lives and are not divorcing reconciliation within their relationship from reconciliation in the Church, as if confession were a purely private matter without connection to the lived reality.

The sacramental action of reconciliation builds upon the acts of reconciliation that take place in your everyday life; it celebrates the reality of God's grace in your life. In the sacramental ministry of the Church, you receive forgiveness from our compassionate God and acknowledge the triumph of God's grace over personal failure.

In the Catholic perspective, where there is sin, there is also the opportunity for grace. The sacrament of reconciliation is meant to be a healing sacrament for both of you. It is designed precisely to deepen your love and care for each other at those moments when you are aware of the fragility of your relationship.

Since Eucharist and reconciliation deal with the most fundamental attitudes you can have toward life, namely, being grateful and being ready to forgive and to ask for forgiveness, interreligious couples will be able to participate in the rites of their respective religious traditions that underline these attitudes. The Jewish observance of the Day of Atonement, for example, places tremendous emphasis on repentance and the reform of life. A Christian married to a Jew will find in the beautiful prayers of the Jewish service for that day both inspiration and material for reflection.

Your love for each other now, during your engagement, has the potential to grow and develop. There is no way your love will remain static if you consider the skills mentioned here and use them consciously and consistently. Do not take your love for granted—and it will be the one place throughout your marriage where you find peace and fulfillment as human beings going about the work of love. Now, during your engagement, is the time to begin building these skills.

Reflecting Together

Successful marriages are the result of a lot of work and attention on a daily basis. Can you add other attitudes and skills that you think are important to the success of an ongoing relationship?

Which psychological skills work best for your relationship?

Which spiritual skills work best for your relationship?

POSTSCRIPT

The single purpose of *Creating Your Christian Engagement* has been to help the two of you live your engagement period as fully as possible. There's no reason why this shouldn't be one of the most blessed periods of your life. It begins in joy with a mutual decision and ends with the joyous public celebration of your wedding. In between, you deepen the affection that binds you ever closer to each other and sets you on a course toward a fully alive marriage. You are indeed very special persons.

Chapter by chapter, we have discussed some of the important areas that you need to pay special attention to as you make your journey toward the altar. The best preparation for marriage is your ability to succeed in dealing with the challenges and opportunities that arise from the interpersonal and practical aspects of your relationship.

We have asked you to reflect on what it means to get married in the Church. Chiefly, it means that your faith will play an active role in your life decisions. It also means that you will be assisted by and supported by those persons who profess faith in Jesus Christ and the liberating gospel he preached. It means you will participate in the sacramental life of the Church, and your marriage will reflect the love of God for the world and the love of Christ for the Church.

We hope that you have many relatives and friends whose lives illustrate this for you. Their lives, not our words, deliver this message in the most forceful way possible. As you prepare the liturgical celebration of your wedding, you will have a chance to bring together your love for each other and your faith. Don't miss this opportunity. It will be a real service to all who witness your marriage.

It has been said that the glory of God is a human being fully alive. If we may take the liberty to adapt this saying, we dare to say, "The glory of God is the flourishing of the engaged couple in love, fully human, fully alive, creating their relationship for the well-being of themselves and for all humanity."

Your engagement and marriage is your great adventure and our great hope.

Blessings and best wishes!

ABOUT THE AUTHORS

John Barry Ryan is a liturgist as well as a professor in the Religious Studies Department at Manhattan College in Riverdale, New York, where he teaches a course in Christian Marriage.

Ryan earned his B.A. in English literature from the Catholic University of America and a M.A. from Manhattan College. He received the Baccalaureate in Theology from the University of Strasbourg, France, and did further theological study at the Institut Liturgique and the Institut Catholique in Paris, France.

Ryan, a founding member of the North American Academy of Liturgy, is author of numerous books and articles and lectures widely on liturgical topics.

Francis J. Lodato, Ph.D., is a psychologist, counselor, and Professor Emeritus of Counseling Psychology at Manhattan College in Riverdale, New York. His articles have appeared in the *New York Times*, *Catholic New York*, *Momentum*, and numerous professional journals on psychology and education. He is also the author of numerous books and a regular religious column.

He received his Ph.D. from St. John's University and has done post doctoral work at Yeshiva University, the New School for Social Research, and the University of Chicago.

Dr. Lodato is also a sports psychologist and serves as team psychologist for the Los Angeles Kings and several other sports teams. He has worked with players on the Miami Dolphins, New York Giants, and Philadelphia Eagles, as well as the Montreal Concordes of the Canadian Football League.